I0035727

Convince Investors to Fund You

The Insider's Guide to
Avoid Deadly Mistakes and Gain
Real Success with Your Startup Business

from GetTheBigYES.com

Tom Marcoux

Spoken Word Strategist
Executive Coach – Pitch Coach
International Speaker-Author of 50+ books
CEO

A QuickBreakthrough Publishing Edition

Other Books by Tom Marcoux:
• Darkest Secrets of Making a Pitch to the Film / TV Industry
• Soar with Confidence: Pitch – Lead – Succeed
• What the Rich Don't Say about Getting Rich
• Time Management Secrets the Rich Won't Tell You
• Relax, You Don't Need to Sell (Make Sales without Being Pushy) … with Authentic Marketing
• Dark Arts Defense Against Toxic People
• Darkest Secrets of Charisma
• Secrets of Awesome Dinner Guests: Walt Disney, Steve Jobs …
• Amazing You … featuring Secrets of Extreme Confidence
• Darkest Secrets of Persuasion and Seduction Masters

Praise for *Tom Marcoux's Methods that Help Entrepreneurs Gain Funding*

• "I'm truly grateful to Tom Marcoux for essential tips that helped me win the Grand Prize of the Pitch Competition—the Igniter Summit in Bangkok, Thailand." – Neeraj Aggarwala, CEO/Founder of Sportido
• "You'll learn to build and sustain a powerful motivation to keep focused and achieve your dreams." – David Barron, co-author of *Power Persuasion*

Praise for Tom Marcoux's Other Work:

• "Concerned about networking situations? Get *Relax Your Way Networking*. Success is built on high trust relationships. Master Coach Tom Marcoux reveals secrets to increase your influence."
– Greg S. Reid, Author, *Think and Grow Rich Series*
• "In Tom Marcoux's *Now You See Me*, the powerful and easy-to-use ideas can make a big difference in your business and your personal relationships."
– Allen Klein, author of *You Can't Ruin My Day*
• "In *Darkest Secrets of Persuasion and Seduction Masters: How to Protect Yourself and Turn the Power to Good*, learn how to defend yourself against manipulation."
– Dr. JoAnn Dahlkoetter, Coach to CEOs and Olympic Gold Medalists
• "In *Connect*, Tom's advice on how to remain true to yourself and establish authentic rapport with clients is both insightful and reality based. He [shows how] to establish oneself as a credible expert."
– Arthur P. Ciaramicoli, Ed.D., Ph.D., author *The Stress Solution*
• "In *Reduce Clutter, Enlarge Your Life*, Marcoux will help you get rid of the physical and mental clutter occupying precious space in your life. You'll reclaim wasted energy, lower your stress, and find time for new opportunities." – Laura Stack, author of *Execution IS the Strategy*

Visit Tom's blogs: GetTheBigYES.com   PitchPowerFest.com

Tom Marcoux

CONTENTS*
* These are highlights. Much more is in this book.

DEDICATION AND ACKNOWLEDGMENTS

This work is dedicated to YOU. Here are Special Offers:

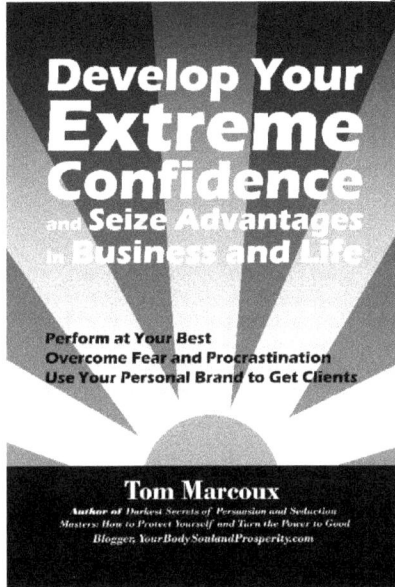

- Get your free eBook *Develop Your Extreme Confidence and Seize Advantages in Business and Life* at http://bit.ly/29bVpox
- Apply for a **Free Breakthrough Strategy Session** with Tom Marcoux https://GetTheBigYES.com/nextstep

This book also dedicated to the terrific Video/Audio Strategist and author Johanna E. Mac Leod. Thanks to Dave Hobley for our conversations. Thanks to Johanna E. Mac Leod for this book's cover. Thanks to my father, Al Marcoux, for his concern and efforts for me … and to my mother, Sumiyo Marcoux, a kind, generous soul. Thank you to Higher Power … and to our readers, audiences, clients, my graduate students and my team members of Tom Marcoux Media, LLC and GetTheBigYES.com. The best to you.

Thank you to the contributors (including interviewees):
LaChelle Adkins
Marc Allen
Dr. David Bergner
Taylor Cone
Jeanna Gabellini
Natalie Glebova
David Joud
Guy Kawasaki
Jay Conrad Levinson
Dr. Frederic Luskin
Andres Pira
Bill Reichert
Danielle Strachman
Dr. Ginny Whitelaw
Henry Wong

Many blessings to you,
Tom

Tom Marcoux
Spoken Word Strategist

Convince Investors to Fund You

Imagine this: it's your big moment. Either you're in front of a crucial audience and you're making the pitch of your life. Or you're sitting across from *the investor* who could launch your dream. Then your mind goes blank. What can you do?

This book, now in your hands, includes answers that I have communicated to audiences from New York to New Zealand (including Silicon Valley, California, Thailand and more). In my workshops *Convince Investors to Fund You* and *Your Secret Charisma: Hidden Methods for Influence and Trust*, I have revealed the secret-methods so that you overcome the tough moments that make or break your pitch or your life-changing meeting.

This book is designed to be a quick read.

We reveal answers to these questions:
- How do I convince investors to fund me?
- How do I create the slide deck that gains meetings with investors?
- How do I handle it, if my mind goes blank?
- How can I use hidden methods to convince the investor?
- What can I do if things go bad in a pitch meeting with an investor?
- How can I experience *real confidence* and gain the trust of investors? (Secrets of Extreme Confidence)

- How can I speak with No Fear?
- How do I show confidence when under fire from an investor's tough question?
- What can I do if I lose heart in my project/company?"
- How can I stay strong and keep going forward in the face of Rejection Trouble?

You'll find great value in how the book includes guidance from **top venture capital leaders** who use their power to say yes or no to startup companies. You'll find guidance from a billionaire, millionaires, top entrepreneurs and more.

You'll learn to avoid *3 Deadly Mistakes* that can torpedo your efforts to gain investors.

These Methods Gain Results:
- "I'm truly grateful to Tom Marcoux for essential tips that helped me win the Grand Prize of the Pitch Competition—the Igniter Summit in Bangkok, Thailand." – Neeraj Aggarwala, CEO/Founder of Sportido
- "Tom Marcoux has coached me to make my speeches compelling and powerful. He has helped me prepare for the media. And, he's helping me prepare my TED Talk. Do your career a big favor and engage Tom Marcoux, the Spoken Word Strategist." – Dr. JoAnn Dahlkoetter, Sports Psychologist, author of *Your Performing Edge* and Coach to CEOs and Olympic Gold Medalists

Let's begin.

Section One

How do I convince investors to fund me?

Countermeasure: Use the 5 C's to create trust.

As he gave a pitch to fifteen investors circling a table, Sam faltered. The next five pitch-makers crashed and burned, too. My heart went out to them. I saw the disappointment on their faces. They knew that they had failed to connect. None of them gained funding.

It was worse. They didn't know what mistakes they made. Seeing such losses inspired me to write two books: *Darkest Secrets of Making a Pitch to the Film and Television Industry* and *Soar with Confidence: Pitch – Lead – Succeed.*

More than that, I created a workshop, *Convince Investors to Fund You,* that has served participants from Silicon Valley, California to Bangkok, Thailand.

Convince Investors to Fund You:
Master the 3 Critical Factors of Pitch,
Network and Follow-Up

At conferences, after I have served as a Pitch Judge, people leading startup companies approach me. I'm glad to be helpful. Some of them come on too strong, and it's clear no one trained them in how to create rapport before they make "the big ask." A realization blossomed in my thoughts: *Investors know on a subconscious mind level that some startup leaders are pros and others are* **amateurs.**

I trust that you've seen that first impressions sometimes cannot be transformed, so it is crucial to do your best to prepare. You need to make an excellent impression on someone who can change your life for the better.

The big idea here is that certain individuals may know how to pitch but crash and burn when it comes to networking and follow-up.

You need to know how to respond if an investor comes up and says, "I'd like to know more about what you're doing."

The truth is that the entrepreneurial idea is not always king or queen. It's whether you are trustworthy. Basically, an investor says, "Yes, I want to go on this adventure with you."

The problem about an adventure is that somewhere along the line you can get hit and bleed.

The investor is saying, "Can I trust you to lead?"

Two Major Ideas Related to Convincing Investors

To convince investors to fund you, hone your skills related to…

• Be heard and be trusted.

• Investors are testing you all along the way.

It's best that investors test the startup leader because they want to know answers to: "Can you succeed? Are you trustworthy?"

Recently, an interviewer asked me, "What's the biggest thing that an introvert could do to just screw up the whole thing?"

"Fail to rehearse," I replied.

In my *Convince Investors to Fund You* workshop, I truly like helping people rehearse *during* the workshop. I recall this quote:

I hear, and I forget.
I see, and I remember.
I do, and I understand.
– Confucius

What Do Investors Want to Know About You so They Find You to be Trustworthy?

In an interview, I said, "Investors want to know that you're trustworthy. And to know that you're stable." That got a chuckle from the interviewer.

Recently, I gave a workshop, *Convince Investors to Fund You* at a Silicon Valley, CA. Conference featuring keynote addresses by Stanford University notables.

This caught my eye because I have taught MBA students at Stanford University twice.

Additionally, I served as a Pitch Judge (for the conference), working with fellow Pitch Judge Henry Wong (a leader with Garage Technology Ventures, co-founded by Guy Kawasaki).

During my workshop, I shared the following "5 C's."

The 5 C's to Assure Investors that You Are Trustworthy
1. Confident
2. Competent
3. Connection-building
4. Conflict-skilled
5. Coachable

1. Confident

To be perceived as confident, you do well to make sure that your words and body language are congruent.

Notice if your words do not match your hand gestures. If you say, "I'm confident that my new XY product will gain a 67% market share in two months"—but you're wringing your hands, there's a real problem. Your wringing hands *communicate your nervousness and self-doubt* more powerfully than your words might imply confidence.

The solution is to pay attention and act in positive ways. If you have a habit of wringing your hands, get your hands away from each other.

If you feel nervous, make sure that you have a 3 x 5 card in your hand and not an 8.5 x 11-inch sheet of paper in your hand. Why? A sheet of paper will betray the trembling of your hand.

If someone asks a tough question, pay attention and avoid your feet unconsciously betraying you by stepping back. Instead, *practice taking two appropriate steps toward the person* and say something like "I can see that's important to you."

The above are just a few examples of how you can make your words and body language congruent—so they tell *one* story. The story is: You are confident. Confidence is contagious.

Here's something I often emphasize:
Confidence is not comfort.
Confidence is a toolkit, and you work it.

2. Competent

When one wants to signal to investors that he or she is competent—particularly in a pitch, it's best to use something I call the B.E.C.C. process.

In a pitch, you communicate with these elements:

B – big idea
E – engage with story
C – credible
C – compelling

Here we'll focus on the Big Idea. My short, memorable way to look at a Big Idea is "Unfair advantage, disruption and big profits." From my conversations with investors, I see that these three elements seize their attention.

The highly competent person delivering a pitch provides the Big Idea early in their pitch.

More than two years later, after I presented my B.E.C.C. process in workshops and speeches in Silicon Valley, California, I had the chance to interview Bill Reichert. I was energized to hear his emphasis on "credible and compelling."

Interview with Bill Reichert

Tom: When somebody makes a pitch, what is crucial for them to do? What must they do positively?

Bill: In order to be effective at pitching, you've got to do three things. And you've got to do them in 20 seconds. First, you've got to be clear about what it is that your business is doing. The investor has to understand your business, your service or product. You have roughly one sentence to *clearly* communicate what business you're in.

Second, you have to be *compelling*. You have to get them to say, "Wow! That's amazing. Tell me more!" There has to be something about what you are doing that is incredibly exciting, that makes you stand out, that will cause your customers to love you. And you have to get this across in one or two sentences.

Third, you've got to be *credible*. There are a whole bunch of ways to communicate credibility. What is the indication that what you're telling me is true?... you're not just blowing smoke. One of the best is some level of third-party validation.

This brand name person or company is a customer or a partner. Convince the investor that you're really different than the alternatives; you're not just more of the same.

You've got to be clear, compelling and credible in the first 20 seconds. Then investors will listen to the rest of your pitch, rather than checking their iPhones.

Tom: What is the big mistake that someone, who is delivering a pitch, must avoid?

Bill: The big mistake is doing the opposite of clear, compelling and credible. And we see it all the time. It broadly fits into the category of *the curse of knowledge*. One VC calls it, "the paradox of brilliance." This is a nice way of saying it. Entrepreneurs live and breathe their product, market and business all the time. As a result, it's sometimes hard for them to appreciate what the person on the other end, the investor, does *not* understand about what the entrepreneur is doing.

A classic example is the entrepreneur who says, "We're going to disrupt the entire home mortgage industry."

There's no content in that statement. This entrepreneur knows what they're doing and is probably excited about it. We know the company is doing something in the home mortgage industry. But we have no idea why *we* should be excited.

The entrepreneur goes on: "Our SaaS platform will transform the industry by automating manual processes and applying AI-based analytics." Intuitively, we get that automation and AI should be good things, but we still don't understand how this is going to transform and disrupt the industry. For whatever reason, entrepreneurs don't appreciate that we don't already know why their company is brilliant. This is a common, broad-based problem: Lack of clarity about what the heck you're doing. I can't tell you how many times I've been a judge at a pitch competition, and, after a four-minute pitch, one of the judges says, "I don't understand what your business is."

Another classic example of this problem is when an entrepreneur starts using jargon or acronyms to describe what they're doing. If you don't know what the acronym means, then you're totally lost.

Here's an example I love. An entrepreneur came in and said, "And unlike any other power electronics device company, we're using *silicon nitride!*" They looked at us like "Isn't that awesome—amazing—incredible?!"

The entrepreneur could not understand our lack of excitement. It was like they were thinking, *Why aren't you jumping up and down and screaming—and pouring money on us because we're using silicon nitride?!*

The entrepreneur did not understand that we didn't appreciate the extraordinarily compelling physics of their technology. This is an inability to bridge the gap between the entrepreneur's expertise and where the audience is. The entrepreneur needs to communicate an understanding of why a novel technology can be the basis of a business or why a particular business model will be compelling to their customers. The entrepreneur needs to understand where the listener is, and bridge the knowledge.

A related difficulty in pitching is that entrepreneurs may be used to pitching to prospective customers, but VCs are not prospective customers. VCs generally don't appreciate the needs the customers have and the context that the customers live in. If you don't make that context clear to investors, they may not appreciate why what you're doing is compelling.

Tom: Knowing what you know now, what would you have done differently?

Bill: (chuckles) I would have bought Tesla. I had the opportunity to be in Tesla very early—before Elon Musk took over. A friend of mine, Nancy Pfund [founder and managing partner of DBL Partners], was trying to convince me why Tesla made sense for a small fund like ours. And I was trying to convince her that she was insane. That this was ludicrous, as a small fund, investing in a car company. She invested, and I didn't. She wound up with Model S number 2, and I didn't.

[Bill and Tom laugh.]

Bill: Another one that I didn't invest in was Lyft—before it was called Lyft. I sat down with John Zimmer, who pitched me on Zimride, and we passed on that.

That's in response to your phrasing the question "knowing what you know now."

Tom: Let me ask a follow-up. What is more of a life lesson for someone who wants to excel, who wants to make an impact?

Bill: Now we're into the baring your soul part of the interview.

Tom: But I'm not Barbara Walters, so you don't have to cry.

[Bill laughs.]

Bill: One of my big life lessons has been to learn when to pick your fights. When I was a callow youth, I spent more time being urgent about asserting what I considered to be the right way or the truth.

I realized by being so urgent and pushing people harder than they, perhaps, wanted to be pushed, I pushed people away—when I didn't need to ... when it wasn't worth the fight. It wasn't worth being right.

This is the lesson that young high achievers need to learn. Because we're brought up in our culture and our educational system to always be right. The educational system puts this ultra-high premium on being right.

Then you're put into the work world where it's really hard to know what is right, but you still have this overachiever/high achiever ethic that *I got to be right.*

This *I got to be right* ethic slowed me down in a few situations.

Finally, I learned, "Hey Bill, you don't always have to be right." And you don't always have to fight for what you think is the right answer. Sometimes, it's not worth the fight. And, guess what, sometimes you're not right. But in school, high achievers learn that "I don't know" is not an acceptable answer. In school, you have to always be right. The educational system focuses on individual achievement and punishes mistakes. It teaches students that there is a defined process for getting it right—for getting a good grade or a good score. But the real world doesn't work that way. The educational system damages our ability to engage in collaborative teamwork and think out of the box.

So, I've learned to pick my fights and how to collaborate better.

Bill Reichert is co-founder and Managing Director of Garage Technology Ventures, a seed and early stage venture capital firm based in Silicon Valley. He is also a Partner at Pegasus Tech Ventures, a global venture capital firm with offices in Silicon Valley and around the world.

Bill and his partners invest in promising emerging technology companies and work intensively with them to help them grow and succeed. Some of Garage's most successful investments include Pandora Media (NYSE: P), Digital Fountain (acquired by Qualcomm), Coremetrics (acquired by IBM), iNest (acquired by LendingTree), and LeftHand Networks (acquired by HP).

Bill brings experience as a serial entrepreneur to his work with portfolio companies. Prior to co-founding Garage in 1998, Bill was co-founder of Academic Systems, a software company funded by Kleiner Perkins, Accel Partners, and Microsoft. Academic Systems became the leading developer of network-based interactive instructional materials for colleges and universities and was acquired by Plato Learning after an IPO. Prior to Academic Systems, Bill was a senior executive at several venture-backed technology companies, including The Learning Company, which was the leading developer of educational software in the United States before its acquisition in 1994, and Infa Technologies, a touchscreen computer company that developed many of the concepts underlying the Newton, Palm, and iPhone devices. Bill also co-founded Trademark Software, which was subsequently acquired by Dow Jones, while in graduate school at Stanford.

Earlier in his career, Bill worked for McKinsey & Co. in Los Angeles, the World Bank in Washington, DC, and Brown Brothers Harriman & Co., in New York. He has authored and co-authored several articles and speeches on entrepreneurship, venture capital, international trade, and monetary policy.

Bill earned his AB in History and Science from Harvard University and his MBA from Stanford University. He is a member of the Council on Foreign Relations in New York, and is a former Chairman of the Churchill Club in Silicon Valley. He is also an Advisor to the Women's Startup Lab, Nordic Innovation House, and the Korea Innovation Center. He lives with his extraordinary wife Michelle and three incredible children in Los Altos, California. You can contact Bill at reichert@garage.com.

To continue with the focus point of being Competent:
A great pitch answers these questions that I call
the 6 W's:
1. What is it?
2. What is the Big Idea?*
3. Who's it for? Who benefits?
4. Why should I listen to you?
5. What's in it for me as the investor?
6. What does this disrupt?
* I focus on the Big Idea as something that includes unfair advantage, disruption, and big profits.

I take this another step forward with the *4 W's of Pushback from the Investor:*
1) Where is the traction?
2) Where is the proof?
3) What's so different about this?
4) What are you going to do if competitors [take a particular action]?

Here is some language to deal the question, *Where is the*

proof? You can say, "We have confirmed ____ through interviews with [focus group, ideal prospective customers and so on]."

Show Your Competence Method #1: **Have the Investor Know You're Pitching to *Them***

As a Pitch Judge for conferences in both Silicon Valley, California and Thailand, I've seen startup founders fail by giving a pitch that sounds like a pitch to the *customer*. That's a big mistake. You must pitch *directly to the investor.* You must assess exactly what the investor cares about. In more than two decades as a professional speaker and member of the National Speakers Association, I have a lot of experience with delighting audience members. What I do is place various elements into my speech that speak directly to the diverse individuals in the audience—something for this person and something for that person …

When it comes to your pitch to multiple investors in an audience, make sure you identify three vital things that can entice investors. Perhaps, one investor does not care about one of those details (for example, sustainability), still you catch the investor's attention with one of your vital points.

Make sure to *directly address the investors* with something like: "As investors, you're naturally interested in a $97 billion market in …."

Show Your Competence Method #2: **Use the *Power of Paper* and "The Next Step is …"**

Many of us have been assured that showing a good slide will prove a point to the investor. Don't count on this. I suggest, when possible, the pitch-maker use what I call *The Power of Paper*. By this I mean, place vital facts and data on paper (even just one sheet) and into the hands of the investors. Say something like: "As you can see on the Facts and Opportunity Sheet in your hands ...."

People believe what they see, not what they hear.
— Grant Cardone

Additionally, make sure that you "make the offer." In sales, that means you "ask for the order."

How do you do this?

Say directly to investors, "The next step is ..."

You can say, "The next step is that we have a conversation after this presentation. I look forward to talking with you."

If you're in the crucial meeting in which you can close the transaction, you can say, "The next step is we take care of the paperwork" — and you put the document in front of the person for their signature.

3. Connection-building

Demonstrate your finesse in building warm connections. Make the investor feel good as they talk with you. How? *Listen.*

Investors need to trust that you know how to build strong relationships. Great CEOs attract great talent and retain that talent. Great CEOs build coalitions throughout the company and with the board of directors.

Now, I'll share a tough time that helped me learn the lesson of the essential nature of connection-building.

A Real-Life Example: Be Careful about Connection-Building

In this example, I note that if you're not skilled with networking, you're going to have serious trouble. And, if you're not adept at follow-up, you're not going to win.

For example, some years ago, I was raising money for one of my first major projects.

Here's how I describe this when I give a speech about it: (lightly edited transcript)

"I get invited to attend a screening of a feature film that was made with independent funding, not from a studio. So, there was an opportunity for me to be very observant. I know these folks are the investors. I should talk with them. I should at least get my brochure into their hand.

Oh, that'll be great. Because I think: They'll see the brochure, and say, "Great idea! Here's my money!"

That's not how it works.

I found each investor at the celebration party. I gave every one of them my brochures. I felt really good. But then I noticed that they all said that they didn't have a handy business card

They said something like: "Oh, just call my office." They were standoffish.

That should teach me something.

They were there to celebrate that they had participated in getting this other film made. They were NOT there to have someone impose upon them. I was not creating good relationships.

Still, I was in my 20s when I was doing this—so it's understandable that I lacked experience and understanding.

The next day I get a phone call from my production budget mentor. He was teaching me how to do the production budget for making my own feature film. But he taught me nothing about how to develop rapport or network with investors.

So, the production budget guy said on the phone, "I need to talk to you this afternoon. I'll meet you at my home."

I agreed.

He had me sit at his kitchen table. He reached into his pocket and pulled out one of my brochures. So, an investor had given it to him. He tossed that brochure on the table.

Then he disdainfully slammed brochure after brochure on that table.

I wanted to melt into to his flooring and <u>just die</u> so I didn't have to think about how embarrassed I felt.

He said, "You will write an apology letter to my business partner." My budget-writing mentor was a co-producer on that film. This embarrassing situation was awful."

This brochure massacre made a huge impression on me that lasts to this day. In fact, one of my first books was titled *Be Heard and Be Trusted*.

I made it my mission to learn how to create good business relationships—relationships built on trust.

How introverts may overcompensate and alienate an investor

Some introverts *come on too strong*. I call this problem "being a bulldozer when networking." This problem can be trying too hard. It's like a pendulum hitting the opposite side—from withdrawn to *too intense*.

Avoid coming across as too eager, overwhelming the investor. Don't be deluded that if you just tell them the idea, they'll be amazed and reach for their checkbook

Here's what is necessary. **Become a great listener.** To get the listening started, you need to ask suitable questions. For example, you could ask, "So, how did you get into investing?"

The investor might reply with something like: "You know, originally I was an entrepreneur, and I started a company. I thought once I have a truly successful company, I'm going to start investing—being an angel investor in other people's stuff. You know, just to keep the cycle going."

You can reply with something like: "Oh. Sounds great. Would you tell me about your first company and what got you excited about it?"

It's all about building rapport. What you need is something called *emotional intelligence.* Daniel Goleman and others have done much work related to emotional intelligence. I saw a quote from a website that reads "We define emotional intelligence as: Recognize, understand and manage our own emotions ... Recognize, understand and influence the emotions of others." (Tomer Strolight, president of the firm that offers this definition).

This definition can be a springboard for our conversation here. Back in my 20s, when I had the snafu of my giving brochures to investors, I demonstrated that I had *not* developed appropriate emotional intelligence yet. I crossed the line as I tried to get investors interested in my feature film at the celebration for someone else's film.

This experience served as a springboard for my studies and getting mentors.

I also learned how to move beyond a traditional viewpoint about "selling." This part of my journey led to my writing the book, *Relax, You Don't Have to Sell* (which served as a textbook at Sofia University, California). In that book, I share the process of "enrolling."

You enroll somebody; you invite them into what you're doing.
I shared the mess I made as a twenty-something person with my first project. I had come on too strong and self-focused with my brochures. That was in line with my then-picture of traditional selling.

Years later, in my book, *Relax, You Don't Have to Sell*, I

note:

Selling is imposition.
Enrolling is invitation.

You invite the person into your world. That's the invitation part. Still, you do some great listening first. Then, the person might be interested in listening to you.

4. Conflict-skilled

"Tell me about a conflict you and your co-founders had and what happened," I said to a young guy looking for investors. He had stepped up to me after I had served as a Pitch Judge at a conference.

He replied, "No. We don't have any conflicts. We get along really well. It's great. Like we're brothers from another mother."

One of my friends in Silicon Valley, California noted a top startup company breaker: *co-founder conflict.*

Until you've had an argument with your co-founder, I don't know if your team will survive. Investors need to know that you're strong and skillful in leading people to a resolution when conflict arrives.

Perhaps, you've noticed how several people like to control things by trying to use email or texts to state their position, and then they refuse to have a seven-minute in-person (or telephone) conversation.

The key to handling problems and conflict within an organization is to keep the channels of communication wide open.
– Anita Roddick

The truth is: Mature adults and good leaders talk to people they cannot stand.

By this I mean, the trustworthy leader, as Anita Roddick

said, keeps the channel of communication wide open.

The Conflict-Skilled Person Knows When to Say, "I'll walk toward you."

The effective leader practices two important skills (among many others):

- Know when to stand your ground
- Know when to say, "I'll walk towards you."

Sometimes, you must hold your ground. An investor might ask, "Have you fired anyone? Have you ever fired a friend?"

If you can say yes to this, the investor often looks on you as a more seasoned professional.

Conflict-skilled Includes Being Able to Say *No* and to Find *the Third Alternative*

Recently, I heard a couple of people talking about *strength of character*. The idea was that a person needs to be able to say no. If that person cannot say *no*, he or she can be pushed around and even "argued into submission."

Even worse, I've seen people push others *to feel guilty*. How? One person says to an abusive father, "Hey, you're insulting me." And then a family member says, "You know that is Dad's way. Why are you causing conflict?"

Wait a minute. Who was abusive?—the father. But the person standing her ground is being dressed down for speaking her truth? This is trouble.

So, in the situation when a family member defends a crazy-maker-father, there is no "nice" solution. Sometimes, you must simply state what is going on ("you're insulting me") and step back—to protect yourself.

In terms of business, if you find yourself with a crazy-maker co-founder, it may be necessary to part ways.

On the hand, a good co-founder will keep talking with you until you both find *The Third Alternative.* Such an alternative is likely different from your first proposal and your co-founder's proposal. Author Steven R. Covey demonstrated the differences between the three alternatives. His example begins a conflict that co-worker have as they share an office. One co-worker wants the window open (first alternative). The second person wants the window closed (second alternative). They talk and find that the person who wants the window closed prefers to avoid having flapping papers on her desk. The other person wants fresh air. **What is the Third Alternative?** It's opening a window in the adjacent office. Fresh air without flapping papers.

The Third Alternative requires continued conversation and creativity.

5. Coachable

Why do you to need prove that you're coachable to investors? Because investors have seen uncoachable people crash and burn and take their companies down with them.

Several investors sometimes see themselves in young people on their way up. Such investors have thoughts like: "Oh, you look like someone who is a 'young me' when I first started. I can save you from so many big mistakes."

It works best if you come across as all three: confident, competent *and coachable.* Some people are "tech-competent" and "people-clumsy."

Instead, a mature businessperson has all 5 Crucial Characteristics: Confident, Competent, Connection-building, Conflict-skilled and Coachable. That's a mature person.

Have a Story About How You Created Great Results by

Being Coachable

Years ago, as a first-time feature film director, I had the opportunity to be coached by veteran actor George Takei (of *Star Trek* fame).

George (Lieutenant—later Captain Sulu—of *Star Trek* feature films) saved me from a bad scene I had written for the feature film I was directing.

When I met him to discuss a role, he proved gracious and warm. I showed him some storyboards. One depicted a scene, with just one light cutting through the darkness, illuminating our hero. He sits at a small table at one in the morning. He sheds a single tear. That teardrop falls into his teacup. As it strikes the surface, the teardrop makes a tidal wave in the tea. An extreme close-up. Slow motion, too.

This imagery sprung from my mind, fresh from directing music videos.

"Uh, Tom?" George asked gently. "Isn't that a bit melodramatic?"

He quietly coached me to reconsider the scene. And, I followed his guidance. *I saved the production money* by cutting the scene at the storyboards stage. We lost no time and no funds to filming a scene I'd likely discard in the editing room.

This has become one of my "I'm coachable" stories.

Now, it's your turn. **Recall a time when you were coached, and you followed the guidance and gained great results.**

How does the investor know you have the traits of a good leader? *The good impression rises from the stories you tell.*

Beware of How Certain CEOs Flame Out

Unfortunately, some CEOs flame out because they're not coachable, and they're not connection-building. They make "bold decisions" that fail because they had *not* devoted effort to building coalitions and support.

Ultimately, the Board of Directors fires them because they're not successful at building connections with the board directors. I refer to this process as a form of "CEO suicide."

What the Start-up CEO Needs to Be Ready For

Often, after I serve as a Pitch Judge, start-up company leaders come up and ask questions.

Some of them just jump in with, "So who do you know who would like to invest in what I pitched?" Sometimes, my thoughts jump to "oh, another amateur." By this I mean, this person did the "amateur" thing of failing to build rapport first. Then they want me to stick my neck out and risk sharing one of my great contacts with someone who is not adept at building rapport and connections.

Still, I strive to be helpful. So, I ask a few questions:
- How much money do you need?
- What have you finished?
- Have you and your co-founders experienced a big disagreement yet?

Many newbies to fundraising choke on the "how much do you need?" question. The solution is to think it through and know multiple levels of money and what you can accomplish.

It sounds like:
- For $200,000, we can get this done …
- For $500,000, we can get this done and ____ and ____ …

About the Question "What have you finished?"

This is a telling question. The savvy start-up leader does well to have a list of three things that he or she has finished. Why? Because we want a company leader who can stick with a project, lead people, complete the project and get results.

Have References

I'll make this detail brief: Have at least three people who say, "Yes. I would definitely work with [him/her] again, given the opportunity."

Demonstrate You're Coachable by Covering Your "Gaps"

We realize that no human being can do the whole thing by himself or herself. The smart leaders look at how they can "cover their gaps." In my book, *Shape the Future, Lead Like a Pro*, I refer to smart leaders as *RoiLeaders* (who specialize in "Relate, Optimize, Intuit).

The RoiLeader demonstrates that they are truly competent by admitting their gaps and hiring people to shore up these areas.

The smartest thing I ever did was to hire my weakness.
– Sara Blakely

Incompetent people either try to cover up a weakness, or they might be delusional and think they do not have any weakness.

The good news is that the RoiLeader is coachable.

The Coachable Person is Trustworthy

When networking, you get people to like you by *listening first*.

The classic idea is that one wants a new person to know you, like you and trust you.

For example, Ross Perot invested in Steve Jobs' company,

NeXT. Perot said that he really was investing in Steve Jobs.

Investors are looking for someone they can trust to lead a company they invest in. Why? Many companies must pivot fast before launch and when the first version of a product gets into the marketplace. The leader must often scramble to energize members to make last-minute changes.

For example, a company had a good plan. They would launch eight products and see what worked. They wisely realized that some products would fail. They were fortunate: Project #2 was the Thighmaster that generated more than $100 million in sales. This was their second project, but they were ready to go through eight projects.

Here's a story that illustrates the pattern of what often happens in the marketplace:

Sandy decides, "I'm going to sell ice cream and people are going to eat with these spoons. Then, Sandy gets surprised. Customers say, "The ice cream is okay, but those spoons! We love those spoons. They're fantastic." Sandy has her company do a pivot.

What's great about small start-up companies is that a good CEO can make a fast decision and jump on an opportunity.

In summary …

Recently, I asked my co-host on my podcast *Introverts Own Your Voice* (on iTunes and YouTube), "What will you take forward from our conversation about the 5 C's?"

She replied: "I think the biggest thing is that the investor doesn't just invest in your project or idea, they're investing in you and your capabilities."

List of the *Five Exercises*

At my workshop, *Convince Investors to Fund You,* I use five exercises. The attendees rehearse powerful actions, and this process transforms their approach to critical situations. Here I will share brief descriptions of the exercises. (Participating in the exercises in-person at the workshop provides the best experience.)

1. **Confident** – Exercise 1
   Congruent-Walk Toward the Question. The purpose of this exercise is to give the workshop attendees the experience of holding their body language in a confident manner even though they're in an uncomfortable situation. They practice saying, "I can see that's important to you" while they walk *toward* the person who asked the question.

2. **Competent** – Exercise 2
   Express the Big Idea. The purpose of this exercise is to practice clearly expressing a Big Idea that captures the attention of investors. Attendees practice expressing their Big Idea with these 3 Elements: Unfair advantage, disruption and big profits.

3. **Connection-building** – Exercise 3
   Positive Small Talk. The purpose of this exercise is to practice asking a question that does *not* feel invasive to the investor—upon first meeting. An invasive question can sound like "What are you looking for in an investment?" That is putting the investor "on the spot." Instead, we ask, when appropriate, a *gentle question* in a friendly tone: "So, how did you get into investing?"

4. **Conflict-skilled** – Exercise 4

Positive Story about Conflict. The purpose of this exercise is to have the workshop attendee practice describing how he or she led a team to a positive resolution of a conflict-laden situation. The pattern is to tell a Positive Story with these elements: "My point is that I'm good at leading people through a conflict situation. For example, the conflict was _____, and I led the positive resolution by doing ____. And the great results were _____." The extraordinary leader ably guides team members through conflict because conflict can often lead to better solutions, better products and better engagement with clients.

5. **Coachable** – Exercise 5

   "Mentor Guided Me" Story. The purpose of this exercise is to help the workshop attendee form and express a story that demonstrates that the person responds well to coaching, takes direction and achieves excellent results. This dispels the investor's concern that the startup leader may be too ego-centered to face reality and learn from others. The pattern is to say something like: "One of my mentors guided me with _____. And when I implemented what they suggested, the great result was ____. My point is: I make certain that I am coachable."

   * * * * * *

Special Notes about Follow-up:
- Be brief.
- Respond quickly and be consistent.
- Devote effort to fulfill what the person has already communicated as important to them.
- Identify what their workstyle preferences are. By this I mean, find out if they prefer email, text,

Skype or in-person meetings and other such details.

To make this memorable, I developed the W.I.N. process:

W – work their workstyle preferences
I – integrate investor's priorities
N – nurture investor's impressions

1. Work their workstyle preferences

It's vital for you to identify as soon as possible the investor's workstyle preferences. You avoid crossing a line and losing the investor. For example, you might encounter an investor who is trying to save his or her marriage and has decided that the hours between 6 pm and 8 pm are only for family.

If you call between the hours of 6 and 8, you may be on the receiving end of the investor's intense anger—even if you hadn't received this information earlier.

Additionally, related to workstyle preferences: Some people prefer email and texting. Others prefer in-person meetings. Some people reserve weekends for their families.

You can get information about an investor's workstyle preferences by asking something like: "When I work with someone, I always like to find out what their workstyle preferences are. And in this way things go smoothly. I don't make an error and call you at the wrong time. Or if you prefer email, I focus on providing what information you need in the way you prefer to receive it."

2. Integrate investor's priorities

It's vital for you to make your communications focused on the investor's priorities. Anything else will be noise or pollution to the investor. On the subconscious mind level, the investor is likely to consider you an amateur. Once that impression takes root, you have a huge problem. The way to get around this is to be sure to ask questions that often take the form of *"What's most important to you about...?"*

3. Nurture investor's impressions

The more you know about the investor's impressions of you, your offering and other pertinent details, you are better able to nurture the relationship.

You can ask questions like:

- What do you like the most about this investment opportunity?
- What do you like the most about investing with me?
- I like to learn. If you had a moment to coach me, what would you bring to my attention? [You create the impression that you are coachable. A classic idea is: "Ask for funding and you get advice. Ask for advice and you get funding."]

Now, Henry Wong reveals the essentials of making a great pitch.

Interview with Henry Wong

Tom: When somebody makes a pitch what is crucial for them to do?

Henry: The pitch has to be clear, precise, and self-explanatory in 25 words. Sometimes, at a cocktail party, you walk up to somebody who may be the CEO or a major partner of a venture capital firm. You say, "I have this project."

The CEO says, "What do you got?"

You have 60 seconds for your spiel, and you have to

---

exactly describe what you do. Clear, precise and crisp.

Tom: What is the big mistake that somebody, who is delivering a pitch, must avoid?

Henry: They don't know what they want. They don't know what they have discovered. They are just not sure about themselves. When one is not sure of oneself, it shows in the language and the delivery of the verbal communication. If you don't know what the hell you're doing, I don't want to fund you. You're kidding me, right?

Tom: Knowing what you know now, what would you have done differently in business?

Henry: I would have been like a machine. If a guy does not fit the department, I would have fired him. Learn how to fire people. Not as bad as Steve Jobs. But learn how to cut the cancer cells away from your company. For example, I was the manager of a bullpen of nine people. They were different types of telemarketers who handled the sales of software.

One guy in the bullpen was so negative. Instead of taking phone calls and making phone calls, he would just walk around and talk to the other people. He was negative—complain, complain, complain. As a manager, I was a good guy. I gave him a verbal warning and two written warnings. I asked, "Do you want to work at this company?" And I didn't fire him. I was so nice. I followed procedure, but sometimes you cannot let the procedure run you. You have to fire the bad apple. It's like the old phrase: One bad apple will spoil the bunch.

Professor Henry H. Wong has been a prolific and successful venture investor, serial entrepreneur, and

Stanford University Mentor in Silicon Valley during the last 38 years.

After working for four Fortune 100 corporations, Henry channeled his entrepreneurial spirit to go and "change the world."

Frustrated with existing sloppy edge technologies, Henry founded, seed-funded, and exited five successful startups, including SS8 Networks (ADC Telecom), IP Communications (Nokia), XaQti Semiconductor (Vitesse), CNet Technology (IPO), and Combinet (Cisco). He was always the founder, chairman, first president, and CEO. Professor Henry has the successful experience in selling his startup Combinet to Cisco for US$165M in 1995 money valuation.

Realizing that "money makes the world go round," Henry founded Diamond TechVentures, a Trans Pacific Venture Investment firm. In parallel, he was also the venture partner to Guy Kawasaki's Garage Technology Ventures, and before that, Crystal Ventures, a Taiwan President Lee's $250M VC Fund.

With the fast growth in Silicon Valley and the ever-changing landscape of technological advancement, a different ecosystem is needed to accommodate growth and accelerate prosperity. To address this, Henry founded TechLAB, an Innovation Center, where he coined the term, "Find it, Fix it & Fund it." Pre-qualified startups or companies that Henry continues to help are incubated inside this accelerator under a secured environment, where the filing of new patentable technologies is done on-site.

The Singapore government's SPRING agency funded Henry's iStartUP program to train Singapore entrepreneurs. The Hong Kong government honored Henry as the "Game Changer" returnees with the Home Coming Tipping Point award. The IT Minister Choi Yanghee of the Korean government recognizes Henry's continuous contribution to their Knowledge Innovation Center (KIC) and named him an Advisor to South Korea.

Henry holds a Business degree from the University of Utah, an MBA in Telecom Management from Golden Gate University. He is an MBA Professor in Sofia University, and is a Mentor in Stanford University. He was a 2002 finalist for the Ernst & Young "Entrepreneur of the Year Award." Henry is a frequent Keynote Speaker, Panel Discussion contributor and a Business Plan Competition Judge.

VIDEO on Professor Henry Wong's Stanford University Lecture: https://bit.ly/2MJhqCT

Professor Henry H. Wong is available as a Keynote Speaker, Business Plan Competition Judge or member of a Panel.

Subject to availability, Professor Wong can provide an in-house training on "From Garage to IPO" customized for Incubator, accelerator, science park, corporate strategic planning department and government agencies. For further details, please email Henry@Garage.com

Or call +1-408-234-6810

Power Principle: Create trust by using the 5 C's: Confident, Competent, Connection-building, Conflicts-killed and Coachable.

Power Questions: How might you fail to give a strong impression that you excel at the 5 C's: Confident, Competent, Connection-building, Conflicts-killed and Coachable? Which people do you trust to help you with your rehearsals? Will you get a coach?

Get Access to Free Videos to Take Your Skills to a Higher Level
Go to GetTheBigYES.com/YourAdvantage

Tom Marcoux

Section Two

How do I create the slide deck that gains meetings with investors?

Countermeasure: Create a slide deck that gains an *Immediate Yes* with the first slide and utilize the investors' *rapid cognition.*

"The slide is too complicated. The eyes don't know where to look," I said to my client, Stephen.

Like a number of clients, Stephen was tangled in details.

Too much detail on a slide creates mud and confusion.

Worse than that: such a slide misses the opportunity to gain an *Immediate Yes.*

By Immediate Yes I mean, that you want the investor to have subconscious thoughts like:

- Yes—this look good; I'm interested
- Yes—this person in front of me is a pro—it's worth listening for 20 more minutes—at least.
- Yes—I'm in! (unless something changes the investor's mind)

Industry pro and original TV Show *Shark Tank* celebrity/investor Kevin Harrington tells the story of giving the shortest presentation. The top real estate investor said, "Don't sit down. Tell me why I should let you sit down."

Kevin responded, "I have something for you that would

take four hours of your time and make you $4 million."

The top real estate investor said, "Sit down."

I share the above example to illustrate how little time you have to impress an investor so that person engages with your presentation or slide deck.

Research demonstrates that people practice *rapid cognition and thin slicing*. To describe this briefly: People make a quick decision on a small bit of information.

Years ago, I gave the speech "First Impressions: The 4-Second Barrier." I do not use that title any longer. Why? It's 2 seconds or less now.

Your first slide must capture the investor's attention in 1 second or less.

The first slide must be simple, compelling and inviting.

Just as important: Customize the slide deck based on the specific type of investor you're addressing. As I work with clients, we develop different slides decks that we color-code. The slide decks differ related to:

- Impact investor?
- Obsessed with sustainability?
- Only interested in TAM (total addressable market) and other financial considerations?

We'll use the GREAT-SIGN Process to help improve your slide deck.

G – give the emotional hook
R – remember *it's a show*
E – engage their eyes
A – ask for what you want
T – tell the story

S – set the meaning

I – identify *The Power of 3*

G – get research to paint the picture

N – Nurture *if-then patterns*

1. Give the emotional hook

The first slide must grab the investor's emotional attention. As I mentioned, you need to get Immediate Yes. Why? Researchers have noticed the effect of *rapid cognition.* That is, people make a decision of yes or no with quite little information.

What are we talking about?

The person decides …

- Yes—this makes sense. I want to know more.
- Yes—I like this person giving the pitch. They seem worth listening to.
- Yes—this is a Big Idea*. I'm interested.

We're talking about how people are moved by emotion then later justify based on the facts. You need to identify what is most important to the investor and then design the first slide to move the person's emotions in your favor.

When I say Big Idea, I focus on unfair advantage, disruption and big profits.

2. Remember *it's a show*

Often as I work with a client, I remind them that in order to get someone to say *yes,* we need to remember this principle: *It's a show.* People respond to entertainment and to that which moves their emotions.

Unfortunately, many novice company founders try to begin their pitch with mere logic, facts, graphs, tables and pie charts. *All of that is support.*

On the other hand, it's reported that Steve Jobs focused on the vital ideas, and he did *not* start with a PowerPoint app as he formed his speeches. Instead, he began with the freedom of using pencil and paper.

Be sure to focus on simple emotion-grabbing elements.

3. Engage their eyes

Choose what you want the investor to focus on *first.*

I say to my clients: "Guide their eyes."

I've developed a process I call the **First Time Viewer Monologue.** I'll look at a client's slide and vocalize what I imagine is flowing through the first-time viewer's mind.

I'm looking to imagine what the first-time viewer is thinking and feeling as they get their first glimpse of a slide.

It sounds like:

"What's this about? Oh, it's an app. What for? To help people ____. That's okay. Nothing special. Is there anything going on here that disrupts the industry? Oh, here's a detail. Why didn't they put that front in center? Are these guys sure about what they're doing? Are they pros?"

I've noticed that several my clients begin with a rough draft of the first slide that is too complicated.

I'll comment: "It's too complicated. Their eyes don't know where to focus. We must direct the investor's eyes to focus on what we want them to see in the first half second that they encounter this slide."

4. Ask for what you want

I've noticed novice company founders faltering during their pitch because they fail to say exactly what they want.

If a founder fails to be forthright and say something like, "We're raising $400,000 and with that we will accomplish these milestones…" investors may conclude that the founder is *not* really CEO material. They may also conclude that the founder does not have a CEO's approach, strength, and trustworthiness. The CEO must lead. To lead you must be able to say, "This is what we need. This is what we want. And this is what we're going to do with these funds."

It's better to say, "For our first round of funding, we need $200,000 to accomplish ____. At the level of half million, we can also accomplish A, B, and C."

I often suggest to clients that offering two levels of your "ask" is helpful because your listener has two choices to entertain.

5. Tell the story

Human beings are conditioned from our childhoods to respond to a story. Every image in the slide deck tells a story if you're doing the process correctly. It's truly important to pull out the meaning and make it clear to the investor viewing the slide. Do not expect the investor to make the leap of logic to know what's most important about a particular graphic.

I've advised some of my clients to show the bar graph and then to use a dialog balloon that states the point in a clear, brief way. It can be a simple statement of: "This opportunity centers on _____, which opens the door for big profits."

6. Set the meaning

Do *not* let your slide be vague. You're the one who must set the meaning. Why? We know that investors spend so little time per slide. How do we know this? When my clients use docsend.com, they have seen data: An investor would spend 4 seconds on one slide and then perhaps 15 seconds on a different slide.

You cannot let the investor potentially come to the meaning on their own. You need to be clear and compelling.

How? Title the slide in a vivid and enticing way.

For a closing slide, this title "Why We Win" grabs attention.

If you use a graph, tell them the crucial point.

You could have the words: "We see that only __% of the target market use this ___ item. Our competitors are missing the opportunity of _____."

7. Identify *The Power of 3*

Frequently, with my clients, I emphasize *The Power of 3.* Avoid having more than *3 key details* in the slide.

It's even better if there's only one main element. You'll find power in a *well-designed question.*

For example, when instructing Stanford University MBA students, I first said, "Women live longer than men."

I noticed a couple of male students in the back of the room with scoffing expressions on their faces.

I then used a question: "Why do women live longer than men?"

To the MBA students, I illustrated that a question gets the viewer to use a different part or his or her brain.

The same pattern can be utilized in a well-designed slide to access the part of the investor's brain that you want to.

You can ask a question that can facilitate the *Moment of Aha.* That's when the investor comes to a sudden realization about a detail.

We focused on bringing things down to the simplest elements. So, I frequently say, "Let's use The Power of 3."

Use the Power of *The Moment of Aha ... The Moment of* **Discovery**
Whether it's your first slide or when you're delivering a

20-second pitch while you're networking with an investor, you really need to facilitate them having an Aha Experience.

You want them to feel: "Oh! Wow! That's new. I never saw that possibility before. That's *good!*"

For example, I recently had an Aha Experience while talking with a friend. He made a comparison between something unfortunate and something *extraordinary*.

His tone was dark and down as he talked about how somebody, "Stephen," did a business transaction, while he was thinking, "I'm trying to get something for the least amount of money that I can."

Then my friend said, "I have a new system in which people have a completely different experience. The people exchange value, but they're doing it in the situation of *full gratitude and full appreciation*. No one is trying to get more out of the other person than they're giving."

Boom! That's when I had the Aha Experience. At that moment, I said, **"I'm writing this down."** I paid full attention. Think of it: *full gratitude and full appreciation*.

Earlier in this book, we noticed that Bill Reichert said that the pitch-maker needs to get the investor's heart beating faster. How do we do that? We facilitate an Aha Moment. But what is this kind of moment? It is often a true *Moment of Discovery*. And what's that about? It can be a moment that is quite fun. It's like a delightful surprise.

On the other hand, if you dump a bunch of data and jargon on the investor, they may feel: "Oh. It's just the same old thing. I've already heard nine other pitches that sound like this."

Become a master of the pitch. Be sure to use the power of the Moment of Aha … the Moment of Discovery.

8.   Get research to paint the picture

Often novice company founders fall into a default setting of self-protection. How? By using a bunch of research to make their point. They're trying to disarm anyone who would ridicule what they're saying.

Certainly, we want to use science, data and verifiable evidence to make our points. However, if you use too much material, you will lose the attention of the investor.

Realize that you need to pick the most important item of data. Then use that datapoint to paint a picture in the investor's mind. You can use a word picture—that's the process of using a few words to create an impression/image in the investor's mind.

9.   Nurture *If-Then Patterns*

Often, an investor will say, "Sure. Send me your slide deck."

This is progress. But it's also an invitation into a big competition.

Your slide deck competes with everything else going on for the investor's life—phone calls, other deals and more.

Your solution is to think things through with **If-Then Patterns.**

When the investor looks at your first slide, questions rise in their mind.

So, we're talking about, IF they have a particular question, THEN you have a compelling answer.

The idea is for the first slide to answer the most vital questions.

While delivering my workshop *Convince Investors to Fund You* in Bangkok, Thailand, I introduced the audience to the 6 Ws:

- What is it?

- What's the Big Idea?
- Who's it for? … Who benefits?
- Why should I listen to you?
- What's in it for me as an investor?
- What does this disrupt?

Be Careful About the Choice of Using "FOMO"

I've had clients say to me, "We should use FOMO to grab the investor's attention." FOMO is *fear of missing out.* FOMO is like a scalpel—a tool that can be used for great good or great harm. Be careful of this technique. Investors can see right through FOMO, and you could break rapport with them.

When talking to venture capitalists, I've heard them say, "I missed out on being an early investor in [Tesla, Facebook, Airbnb, and so on.]"

So, how do we tap into their concern about missing the next big thing?

As I work with a client, I frequently do what I call a *Solo-Reflection Session.* During that time, I am alone and I'm thinking about how I can help and guide the client to move forward faster. I also access my intuition during a Solo-Reflection Session.

Recently, during my Solo-Reflection session, I sent an email to a client with this material:

"During my Solo-Reflection session about your company, I was thinking about your comment about invoking FOMO—of course, fear of missing out.

The essence of that process is to use a *comparison* and imagery on the slide that is undeniable and visceral.

Similar to how we have different colored slide-decks for the level of the investor, we can use a number of different FOMO slides.

What do you think and feel would be the undeniable and visceral components for ...
- the sustainability-compelled investor?
- any other impact investor?
- the "big opportunity" investor?
- the "I like to brag" investor?
- the "I am so savvy" investor?"

Be careful about FOMO. **Any investor might become irritated if they think you're being manipulative.**

As I mentioned, FOMO is like a scalpel. It's a tool that can do great good or great harm. Make sure you're ready to deescalate the situation by saying something like: "Forgive me. I was just so excited about _____. Could we back up a few steps?"

A Word about "Using Techniques"

One can torpedo a good interaction with an investor by using a technique in a clumsy manner. Some people are deeply concerned about using *any* technique because they want to *avoid* coming across as "slick and phony."

My response is: Techniques are like a language. It's valuable to learn the vocabulary of *communication that creates connection.*

When I was recently in Thailand to give workshops (*Convince Investors to Fun You* and *Power Time Management: More Time Less Stress, Zero Procrastination*), I learned some Thai words. Women use the word "ka" which shows respect and politeness. Men use a different word that also begins with a "k."

My point is: It's great to know techniques like it's great to know vocabulary.

Here's what counts: Start with a positive intention. Be

sure that you will make your offering into a great value for the investor, too.

Danielle Strachman gives us some insights about being careful of FOMO and the use of other techniques …

Interview with Danielle Strachman

Tom: When somebody makes a pitch, what is crucial for them to do?

Danielle: For 1517, I think we operate a bit differently than other venture funds. One of the things I would say is crucial about making a pitch is that it's really about building a relationship with an investor. Often, when we're working with a founder, since we work with students a lot, it's really more about getting to know the person.

I often say, "A founder will pitch to us when the time is right. But often, we've worked with that founder for months or even years in helping to mentor them and give them some advice on what they're doing."

It's important in a formal pitch to have thought out all the key areas, but even better is to build a relationship with the person they're going to pitch to. Understand the firm and what their interests are, and really find that alignment. Because you don't want to pitch to a group and find out— "Oh, you only do B2B SAS, and I'm Consumer."

We all have limited time and energy, so you want to make sure you're focused in the right places, with the right people. Avoid thinking that this is an investor and it's going to be an automatic fit.

Be sure to get to know the firm, find out what their thesis is, how you fit with that. Keep drawing back to these details in your pitch, because it's about strategic partnership.

Tom: When people are getting to know each other, what helps to build the relationship—and trust?

Danielle: I feel mission alignment is really important. So, if you're working on something that is also important to the other person, this is something that garners the building of the relationship.

Trust is garnered over time. One reason we do a lot of relationship building at 1517 is that anybody can have three good meetings with somebody—in the span of a couple of weeks. This may be what people are used to, when thinking about doing a pitch. But trust comes in when you work with someone over time and you can see: "Hey, this founder or VC—it goes in both directions—did what they said they were going to do. They added value in this way."

We notice if a found owns to when their expectation of goals they would hit fell a bit short. That's really how you build that trust.

You get to see how people work over time—and how much their word matches up with what is actually happening.

Tom: What is a mistake that one might make when building a new relationship with an investor?

Danielle: Going back to what you said about trust. One of the meta-things we look at is how a founder drives the process if they're looking to close out in a week or a month.

For example, we had a team that we went into diligence with. This team was working on a very interesting problem. Due diligence was going great. We did a customer call—that was wonderful.

Everything was wonderful except for this one piece,

which was how the founders were interacting with us to do the sale of their company. The founders were really driving things, using FOMO [fear of missing out] tactics. They said, "Hey, if we don't hear from you by Friday, we're going to have this term sheet from somebody else."

At our stage, the pre-seed stage, somebody else might set terms. But it's not like a Series A Round when somebody takes 80% of the round, and it's over. At this stage, the checks are more collaborative. People are coming in for 10% or maybe 15% of the company at most. We're working with smaller amounts of capital. The risk appetite is high, but you also have to distribute that risk.

When we have had founders, who had sales that were not genuine and their approach was based on manipulative techniques, we said *no*.

We'll go back to the example of the team that had one piece that caused trouble. I returned to that team and I wrote a long piece of feedback: "Listen. I really liked everything. But one thing that has really put us in the No camp was your leadership ability and your ability to walk us through this process. Because one of our core beliefs is how people are in one context is how they are in all contexts."

So, if the person is using spammy, infomercial techniques like "act now"—everything is fast—that's probably how they will treat their employees, how they work with customers and things like that. We look at the situation from a higher bird's eye level of "would we want them doing this with other people as well?"

I said to the team, "It would have been authentic for us to hear something that is really happening. Maybe you have an engineer that you want to hire and if you don't close by Friday, you're going to lose out on that person."

There *is* real pressure that happens in this business. But

I'd rather hear about that, instead of FOMO tactics to get us interested. I'd rather build our relationship up based on what you really need, not from smoke-and-mirrors and fakeness. **So, that's a big mistake that people will make: Their sales process isn't authentic.**

Another mistake is people focus too much on the Total Addressable Market and not enough on the Go-To-Market Strategy.

We have invested in a company that had one of the worst pitch decks I've ever seen. People asked, "Why would you invest?" It's because of the relationship we built with the founders.

I say that people are always more dynamic than a 2-D deck on what they're doing.

One team, for their app, had their Total Addressable Market as all cell phone users. That's just really sloppy. That's probably the sloppiest we've ever seen.

When it comes to Total Addressable Market, you're trying to get a big number on a slide. The piece of that market you might *get* is divided by some number between 2 *and 100.*

But what matters to us, when we're putting that money in, is really your Go-To-Market Strategy. Who do you have a pilot with? How are you going to saturate a group enough to get to the seed stage when you'll go to real contracts and past the pilot stage? That's the nuts-and-bolts strategy that we want to really understand.

First, we want to understand that the market could grow to a certain size. But we really want to know about where you'll get started and how the capital you're taking in now will be used to do that.

Those are two common areas that we see as mistakes.

Tom: Excellent. Because of your insights about FOMO,

I'll include this interview in my book in the section about FOMO. I write that investors can see through it, and it can be irritating.

Danielle: It's *so* irritating. But to be generous, first time founders are facing that it's hard out there.

On the trust side, I see that some founders use the FOMO tactics because the investor side is not well-known for being forthright. It may be that founders have been left with a bad taste in their mouths, and maybe that's why people use certain tactics. I think that it goes back and forth.

For our fund 1517, we try to be transparent and forthright. As pre-seed investors, we know what it's like since we're raising our own funds. We have sort of a different ethos than maybe bigger, more capitalized funds.

Tom: Knowing what you know now, what would you have done differently.

Danielle: One thing is to have started the fund earlier. We started the fund because my colleague and I were running the Thiel Scholarship program. Two years into the program, we had this inkling that some of the young people we were working with would have some big opportunities for them. At that time, we didn't know what it was like to run a fund or to be investors.

So, five years in, we had a number of companies that were starting to do really well. For example, Oyo Rooms [now India's largest hospitality company]—the founder's initial concept was like Airbnb in India. We would take calls with the founder and he would be in somebody's home. The founder would say, "This couch needs pillows." It was all this little nitty-gritty stuff. Today, his company is worth $5 billion in market cap.

From watching people like this founder start to grow, we

thought there is a case to be made to start a fund. If we had started the fund in year three, we could have been more instrumental to those founders.

That is really "crystal ball work." With what I know now, of course, I would have started the fund earlier!

A more practical answer [to the question, *Knowing what you know now, what would you have done differently?*] relates to giving feedback. I'm working on this all the time. Giving feedback, especially if it's negative, is really hard. But as an investor, you need to be really good at doing it.

You need to give negative feedback with people who are pitching you, or with your own portfolio. You have to have these tough-love conversations. You say, "I notice that your company seems to be going off the rails in this way. We don't like that X, Y or Z is happening."

I've learned to be a bit more brazen with giving negative feedback. My colleague and I come with a humanistic approach of everyone is where they're at. At the same time, in working with younger founders over the last ten years, we do have a lot of insight. We have the sense of when things are not going the way the founders want.

Sometimes, delivering that hard feedback is difficult. And, we do it. But sometimes, I wish we did it a bit earlier. That is a practice for us to be better as investors and better in our work with founders.

It's important for founders to know that starting a company and getting investors is a really long-term game, and you're building relationships. So, if you meet with people and you don't like them, I recommend *not* working with them. It's a long, long game, and you want people who are backing you and who are enthusiastic. At the very early stages, you don't want to be afraid to call them at 10 o'clock at night and say, "Hey, here's this thing that is going on …"

It becomes different as people and their company mature to Series A, and you have a board. There's a correct way to run a board meeting.

For your first check in, believer-types, you want them to be going to bat with you all the way.

Tom: Would you like to add something?
Danielle: In terms of tactics that can *fail* … Some people have come across an idea of using touch to build rapport. But it comes across as creepy and weird. I feel, "Stop touching me—this is a professional conversation." People try all kinds of things

Tom: I hear you. Some people get too technique-oriented.
Danielle: Yes!

Tom: —as opposed to showing up genuine and present in the moment.
Danielle: Those are the skills they need to practice—to be genuine and in the moment—instead of "I'll hand the person a hot drink and that will make them feel better about me." I guess there's research that says that these things work. **But it has to be done in a genuine way** and *not* in a contrived way.

Danielle Strachman is a cofounder and general partner of 1517. She has worked with young entrepreneurs for about a decade. In 2010, during the founding of the Thiel Fellowship, Danielle joined to lead the design and operations. She's worked with some of the most prestigious founders like Vitalik Buterin and Ritesh Agarwal. Previous to her work with Peter Thiel, Danielle founded and directed Innovations Academy in San Diego, a K-8 charter school serving 400 students, with a focus on student-led project based learning and other alternative programs.

Danielle Strachman emphasized that one needs to learn to be genuine and in the moment, when interacting with an investor. Now, Dr. David Bergner shares insights about how to develop one's communication skills to foster genuine connection.

Interview with Dr. David Bergner

Tom: What is crucial for someone to do to communicate well?

David: To communicate well, you need to know why you're communicating.

For example, early in my career, particularly at NASA, I would make the implicit assumption that the communication was all pragmatic. We were doing something, and we wanted it to work. If you had information that was valid, that was good. If you had ideas that might work, that was good. The goal was to solve the problem or accomplish the project we were undertaking.

I would call my approach at NASA—pragmatic communication. You have an intersection of what you're doing and what you care about that causes you to communicate. And, others have a similar intention. This is very practical. Being right and being correct are what matter. Having useful ideas is appropriate.

But I realized I would step on people's toes, and I found that how people felt was what really mattered. Communicating related to feelings is something I call the *affective aspect.*

So, when you're communicating, you have both the *pragmatic aspect* and *affective aspect.* To be effective, you need to keep track of those two things and make sure that you really understand what's going on. You need to understand what the person you're talking to really needs. What that person really cares about will include the problem you're trying to solve. But it may also include their own feelings and their own ego. This is where respect comes in, and disrespect can be perceived. In such a case, that person may not care whether you're right or whether your ideas are good unless you make them feel good. Or, if you make them feel bad, they are likely *not* to care whether you're right.

My friend, Somik Raha, has built on the work of Robert S. Hartman. Somik says that some of the things you value are countable. This is the pragmatic end. These are our preferences—things we can place numbers on and say that we have or haven't achieved them. That's *the realm of the head.*

The realm of the heart relates to the affective – things we can describe that we really care about, but perhaps they are not that easy to describe and virtually impossible to count.

The deeper dimension of value clarity in Somik's formulation is *intrinsic values.* And I call this dimension the soul.

So, you have the head, heart and soul.

You can look at what people are trying to do and what they care about—but there is a slightly deeper dimension called *the frame.* You ask, "How is this thing being framed?"

You can look deeper than what they're counting or what they're describing as what they care about. You look at a deeper dimension—a process Thich Nhat Hahn refers to as ***deep looking.*** You get your head out of the way a bit. You watch your emotions but avoid succumbing to them. In this state of being, you can just pay attention. In this process, you can sometimes get deep insights. You get in touch more deeply at the level of the human soul. That is opposed to merely counting.

When you want to communicate well, you might be dealing with a challenging situation. When you turn your attention to the souls involved, rather than the words or things people are counting, sometimes you can get to where the solution to the problem really is. To communicate well is to recognize the head and the heart—and find out where you are. And, when necessary and appropriate, go deeper and recognize these preferences that are being shared are *manifestations of who the person is.*

Here is an example. I sat in a coffee shop in Menlo Park (California), talking with Somik about a model I have called *The Decision Wheel.* A woman came over, and she exuded humility and asked, "How many gallons of gas fit in my car's gas tank?"

"What kind of car do you have?" Somik began.

"You don't have to worry about it," I spoke at the same time. "It will stop automatically." I was referring to automatic function of the gas pump at the nearby gas station.

"Oh, it will stop automatically," she said. "So, I don't have to worry about how much gas fits in my tank. Thank you."

After she left, Somik looked at my diagram of the Decision Wheel that was laying on the table and said, "You just used Question-Decision Duality. We just talked about that. She asked how big her gas tank was, and you inferred that she had a value at stake, and she was deciding what to do. And that value would have been that she doesn't want her gas tank to overflow, and you gave her the information she really needed."

"And not only that, Somik," I said. "I think she just lost her husband."

Tom: Oh! ...

David: And Somik thought that was a little farfetched that I would jump to that conclusion. And, I showed him on The Decision Wheel, when you move from the hard side to the soft side you get "Where is this coming from? Why is that question there?" and then if you look deeper, you may find something important.

About ten minutes later, Somik and I were finishing our coffee. She came over and said, "I'm really so sorry to have bothered you. I just lost my husband—and he used to fill the gas tank."

Tom: ... wow...

[Moved by the tragedy, both David and Tom take a breath at this moment.]

Tom: What should one avoid, in terms of a mistake that would prevent one from communicating well?
David: Based on what I shared ... Avoid talking to someone's head when you need to be talking to their heart—or avoid the reverse of that situation. Also, be sure to recognize that people caught up in projects are really expressing *a part of their soul*—in some way. Or the problem may be that they're *failing* to express their soul.

Additionally, we can avoid missing the opportunity to really connect. For example, I saw this visiting poet, who was a visiting artist at Villa Montalvo in Saratoga, CA. She was clever. Her use of language was excellent. The poems were definitely professionally done, but they didn't touch me. After about twenty minutes, I had some stray thoughts about doing something else.

Later, I mentioned this to my brother, who attended the event with me. As a poet, he said, "In order to touch someone's heart, you need to reach deeply enough into your own."

And, we didn't sense that she had reached deeply in her heart to produce these poems. They were poems of the head.

So, along those lines, let's realize that excellent communicators use the three dimensions of head, heart and soul. Excellent communicators who stand out, like Gandhi or other notable leaders, reach people's hearts and who they are.

You can come from the heart and describe your feelings. But the soul is deeper, perhaps, indescribable. It's a sublinguistic nature of who we are. So, the stellar communicators who deal with the intense problems we face are those who can reach deeply into their own souls to know why they're doing what they do—with complete value clarity. They look deeply enough into others around them to know how to touch their souls or to find those aspects.

Tom: Knowing what you know now, what would you have done differently?

David: I've reflected on this. And, in a meeting at Sofia University where I teach and lead the MBA program, I was listening to Robert Frager as he said, "We should always treat every student with unconditional positive regard."

About unconditional positive regard … at one point I was doing some research at the Center for Design Research at

Stanford University. Some of people there were studying emotion. One of the graduate students was trained to be an emotion coder. One of the emotions is called "contempt." When I thought of contempt, I considered it to be deep hatred. But it can actually be mild—like when you roll your eyes while someone speaks. I thought, as a leader, "I hope I never do that."

A couple of days later, while conducting a staff meeting at NASA, I found myself rolling my eyes after one of my Branch Chiefs shared something. I realized, "I just did that. I just did contempt." I saw others roll their eyes. I became truly sensitive to these expressions.

So, knowing what I know now, I want to avoid expressing contempt, even in its mildest forms, to treat every person with unconditional positive regard. And I want to communicate effectively with the three dimensions of head, heart and soul.

Dr. David Bergner is an energetic organizational leader, accomplished technologist, and passionate teacher with a strong commitment to his students. He retired from NASA with 30 years of diverse experience in science, engineering, technology research and development, program formulation and management, executive management, and organizational development. He teaches courses in Quantitative Methods, Operations Management, and Decision Sciences at Sofia University in Palo Alto, CA, where he is Chair of Business Programs. His decision science approach emphasizes dialogue processes for effective inquiry, balanced with contemplation and reflection, to clarify values, surface assumptions, and develop an appropriate frame. With this foundation, mathematical modeling and data science can generate insights by focusing inquiry on essential variables and facilitating collaborative deep reasoning. David's research interests include frame analysis, computational dialogue models, organizational and team factors in data mining, and the emergence of online decision support communities.

https://www.linkedin.com/in/davidbergner

Principle: Your slide deck must create an *Immediate Yes* in the investor—with the first slide.

Power Questions: What are the different types of investors I am reaching out to? How can I categorize the different types of investors and customize slides that would seize such investors' attention?

Reminder:
Get Access to Free Videos to Take Your Skills to a Higher Level
Go to GetTheBigYES.com/YourAdvantage

Section Three:

How do I handle it, if my mind goes blank?

Countermeasure: Rehearse *Recovery Methods* so you create the impression that you are confident and competent.

In over 20 years of serving as a professional speaker, I've learned that having poise when one's mind goes blank is a matter of strategy and rehearsal.

You can use Recovery Methods to ensure that you avoid looking like a deer caught in the headlights.

Recovery Methods include:
a) "At this moment I want to emphasize …"
b) "I see that's important to you."
c) "I need a pause for a moment. I want my response to be valuable to you."
d) Take a drink of bottled water

Rehearsing Recovery Methods, for even just 9 minutes each morning, will give you an advantage. Your nervousness before a speech will be reduced because you know that you can handle the moment of your mind going blank.

You know how to recover and continue with poise and confidence.

Power Principle: Rehearse *Recovery Methods* so that you appear *confident and competent* if your mind goes blank or if you're given a horrible question.

Power Questions: How will you rehearse the Recovery Methods?
The methods include:
- "At this moment, I want to emphasize …"
- "I see that's important to you."
- "I need a pause for a moment. I want my response to be valuable to you."
- Take a drink of bottled water

Avoid these *3 Deadly Mistakes* —and Gain Investors

Throughout this book, I cover various mistakes and related solutions. At this point we are deep enough into this book to call out *3 Deadly Mistakes.*

1) Failing to Listen
Recently I was at a networking event, and I saw a venture capitalist, "Sam," accosted by an eager entrepreneur. I was stunned at how this person failed to listen to Sam. Sam even shared a look with me. Sam's message was "Oh, no. Another amateur, somebody wasting my time."

The solution here is to listen carefully. Often, a potential investor will ask you a question that will give them exactly what they're looking for. They ask, "What's your traction?" A good response is: "Our traction is …" It helps to repeat a couple of exact words the investor uses.

At every moment investors are testing you. If you fail to demonstrate that you're a good listener, you demonstrate that you are likely an inept leader. Great leaders listen to team members, board members and investors.

2) Failing to Bounce Back Well from Rejection

With all the top people I've interviewed, one fact comes up again and again: Successful people face more rejection every week than other people do. So, a successful person learns to develop strategies to handle rejection.

Learn to instantly reframe a rejection-situation in your thoughts. For example, if an investor says, "No, that's not a match for what we're looking for," you could guess and think that you just received a brush off. However, the truth may be that investor merely has a slot to fill that does not match your venture.

Avoid losing your personal energy needlessly. Look for data points. If the investor winced when you mentioned the unique benefits of your venture, note that. However, realize that this one data point is still not enough to form a complete picture. I've guided clients with a phrase: "Notice if you're just making up stories." Taking a data point and falling into a totally negative impression or story can be counterproductive. For example, one of my clients could not get a particular investor to return her calls. She said, "He doesn't like me. I bet he thinks my idea is stupid." I replied, "Let's observe. It doesn't look like you have enough data points. Until then …" She replied, "I know. 'I'm just making up stories.'" Then she smiled. She avoided losing personal energy.

Years ago, when I was auditioning for acting roles, I had a journal in which I wrote down notes after each audition. I noted *What Worked* and *Areas to Improve*. Once I took those notes, I closed the journal. I felt good because I had done my job with an audition.

You can do a similar action. You can write in your own journal about how each investor meeting turned out. You identify what you did well—*what worked*. Additionally, you identify what you need to work on *to improve*.

Remember, this powerful word when you run into rejection—Next!

3) Failing to Rehearse for When Things Go Wrong

If you get flustered in a conversation with an investor, you lose.

Here's a brief list of things that can go wrong:

a) your mind goes blank

b) the investor doesn't believe that your traction is real

c) in the middle of your giving a brief pitch, another person interrupts the conversation

d) the investor criticizes or even ridicules any aspect of your venture

As I work with my clients, I take them through a process I call *Directed Rehearsal*. I have directed feature films and videos. My focus is on getting people to perform at their best. In order for my client to perform at their best, I direct them, and they rehearse for when things go wrong.

During *Directed Rehearsal*, I have called out to my client, "Your mind just went blank." The client then rehearses one of five Recovery Methods so he or she comes across with poise and skill.

Further along in this book, we will cover more details about how to deal with similar situations when things go wrong. Realize that simply rehearsing the text of your pitch is not good enough. You must rehearse your message and how you will recover when things go wrong—so that you come across as skillful and trustworthy to investors.

Section Four

How can I use hidden methods to *convince* the investor?

Countermeasure: Guide the investor so they can convince themselves.

Frank Greene, a venture capitalist, and I had a discussion about pitching over breakfast one day, some years ago.

"It's important to engage in a *dialogue* with an investor. You can do that even during a pitch to a room of investors," I said. "Answering one investor's question and responding to that *one person* can make a big difference."

"That's true. But they [pitch-makers] don't want to have a dialogue. They just want to pitch," Frank said.

I'll now shared some "hidden methods" so you can build real trust with investors.

We'll use the A.I.M. process:

A – align your listening and dialogue
I – intensify how they convince themselves
M – maximize "what has to happen?"

1. Align your listening and dialogue

As I mentioned, having a good dialogue with an investor, even from the stage, is truly valuable.

A special element of the dialogue includes your skill as a good listener …

Learn Secrets of Great Listening

Have noticed how you feel better when you notice someone listening attentively to you?

Investors, like all of us, want to know that they're being heard.

Listening well pays respect to the other person.

You can use a powerful source of personal charisma when you master some secrets of great listening.

I have written a number of books about charisma including *Darkest Secrets of Charisma, Your Secret Charisma* and *Create Your Best Life: Unleash Your Charisma and Confidence to Change the World.*

I've given speeches emphasizing how *we can get beyond limiting beliefs and thoughts about what charisma is.*

I've broken down the concept of charisma into three different forms:

- *Magnetic Charisma:* A person has a stereotypically attractive appearance that pulls people to them. They walk into a room and people stop and stare. (Some people have a resonant voice that is magnetic, too.)
- *Natural Charm Charisma:* Some people create a warm interaction because they are natural and **good listeners**. That's charming. Some people have a warm smile that creates harmony and a heart-to-heart connection. The other person in the conversation naturally wants to cooperate with the person exuding Natural Charm Charisma.
- *Warm Trust Charisma:* This person has moved distractions out of the way so people can trust them sooner. This person demonstrates in action

that they can be relied upon. Even in a conversation, you can rely on the person with Warm Trust Charisma to pay attention to you and to put effort into understanding what is important to you.

Enhance Your **Warm Trust Charisma** *by Becoming A Great Listener*

What makes a great listener? That's when someone is not shackled by 3 Deadly Mistakes that I call *Listening Blockers*.

Listening Blockers:
1) Defending
2) Judging
3) I've Been There—One Up

1) Listening Blocker: "Defending"

If you came home and were confronted by a loved one who complained: "You never take out the garbage," how would you react?

Many of us would say, "That's not true. Two weeks ago, I took out the garbage!"

What is that comment? It's part of *defending* yourself.

It seems reasonable, right?

Here's the point: Defending is *not* listening.

Instead, devote extra effort to calm yourself down and demonstrate that you're really listening.

Imagine if you could say, "I hear you. It sounds like you want me to help more with the chores. Do I have that about right?"

Can you picture how the family member might begin to cool down?

The essence of Warm Trust Charisma is that people feel

good in your presence when they feel they can trust you.

Here's an example:

> *Matilda:* "Joe, you never take out the garbage."
>
> *Joe:* "I hear you. It's seems like you're frustrated that I haven't taken out the garbage yet. Is there something special happening?"
>
> *Matilda:* "You remember that my Book Club group is coming over tonight. It's Thursday."
>
> *Joe:* "Oh, right. I'll move this garbage out now."

The idea is that Joe avoided defending himself.

Ultimately, Matilda wants to feel that Joe cares about her. How does he demonstrate that? He listens.

2) Listening Blocker: "Judging"

Judging is something that we all do naturally. Our ancestors who survived to pass on their genes were those who paid close attention to negative things in their environment. The ones who did not pay close attention did *not* live to pass on their genes. So, it's natural that we judge everything to make sure that we're safe. We judge someone's words, idea, facial expressions, all of it.

When you're judging, you're *not* listening. You'll need to pull yourself back from judging.

3) Listening Blocker: "I've Been There—One Up"

The third listening blocker is a real challenge because a lot of us were taught the way to show that you empathize or you understand something is to say, "I've been there" or "yeah, me, too."

Here is an example. When I first began as an instructor at a particular university, I sat in the faculty lounge, and a professor came over to me. He said, "How many classes are you teaching?"

"Four," I replied.

"I'm teaching seven classes." That was like he was playing "one up." You might call it "three up" (three more classes).

I adapted in the moment and said, "Wow, you're tough. That's amazing."

The point is that the person has turned the spotlight of the conversation away from my thoughts and to something that seems like it is self-aggrandizing.

Here's another example: Mark comes into work and looks tired. He says, "I've got this newborn."

"I can relate to that. I have newborn twins," George says. That's one up, again.

When the spotlight of the conversation goes away from the person who's talking, that person feels abandoned. The opportunity for a real connection is lost.

I illustrated this once in a speech. I said, "Maybe, you've experienced how a parent might say, 'When I was your age, I had to *crawl* in the *snow* on my *knees* ... and ... I had no pants."

When someone does *I've Been There—One Up*, they're *not* listening. On the other hand, when you listen, you create Warm Trust Charisma. The person trusts you because you're really *with* them. They know you are being respectful and you're paying attention to their concerns.

Use the Solution for Defending, Judging or *I've Been There—One Up*

If you notice that you are defending, judging or using *I've Been There—One Up*, pause. Take a breath. Then ask a gentle question:

- Wow, that sounds intense. So, what did you do

next?

- Oh, that sounds frustrating. How would you like things to go better?

A *gentle question* is one that is easy to answer. It might even be fun to answer such a question.

When you ask a gentle question and listen, you demonstrate that you are holding the space with care for the other person to express himself or herself.

You notice that I used the phrase "Oh, that sounds frustrating." I call this a *Reflective Reply.*

You're reflecting to the person some acknowledgement of their feelings.

You say things like:

- oh, that sounds frustrating.
- That sounds intense.
- That sounds like it was disappointing.

When the person hears your Reflective Reply, he or she *feels heard*. This so important that I wrote a book titled *Be Heard and Be Trusted*. And, this book includes some classic material from that previous book. I'm celebrating 20 years of my focus on building communication that fosters trust. Trust is built on good listening.

So, create that connection. Create that rapport. Create that harmony. *Create Warm Trust Charisma.*

2. Intensify how they convince themselves

The truth is: The more you push, the more the investor pushes back and gives you resistance.

Instead, you'll better by asking questions. Guide the

person to share with you what is most important to them.

You can ask:

- For you to know that an investment is a match for you, what has to happen?
- What makes a startup company a real good candidate for your fund to invest in?
- What matters most to you when you're considering a startup company to invest in?

The point here is to make your comments relevant to the investor. More than that, make sure to appropriately listen and stay silent at times. Let the person think through and feel their feelings so they can convince themselves of the value of your startup business.

Be aware that you avoid pushing.

Instead, invite them into your world and guide them to experience your offer as something that really works for them.

3. Maximize "what has to happen?"

Here's another version of the "what has to happen?" question:

"In order for you to know there's something you want to invest in—what has to happen?"

At that point, the investor could become your "coach." How?

The investor could say, "The startup founder would need to show me traction that means something to me."

You might ask, "How would that look?"

The investor says, "The first clients belong to a group what would be part of a Total Addressable Market of _____."

In summary, you do a process of using "hidden methods" when you make it easier for the investor to convince themselves of the value of your offer.

Power Principle: Guide the investor so they can convince themselves.

Power Questions: What elements of your startup business are most attractive to investors? How can you facilitate that the investor really connects with positive feelings about your company?

Reminder:
Get Access to Free Videos to Take Your Skills to a Higher Level
Go to GetTheBigYES.com/YourAdvantage

Section Five

What can I do if things go bad in a pitch meeting with an investor?

Countermeasure: Use the process of shifting the conversation out of an awkward moment.

Recovery Methods for a Tough Pitch Meeting

Often, I work with clients who are going into a tough pitch meeting. They were given a "warm referral" and a lot is at stake. They do not know what the investor might throw at them. Additionally, if they make big mistakes in the meeting, they might lose the person who gave them the referral.

We use the SHIFT-NOW process:

S – set their permission
H – hear their *leaning* this way or that
I – invite them to share their take
F – focus on "forgive me"
T – target "what is working for you?"
N – nurture and pivot on "I'm curious"
O – open a story
W – work in the mutual friend

1. Set their permission

It's important to put the investor at ease. We get their permission (when appropriate). It could be as simple as asking, "How about we start with the XY section?"

2. Hear their *leaning* this way or that

Several of my clients have been concerned about avoiding the loss of an opportunity. What if you make the wrong guess and you say, "So, you're going to invest in my company, right?" And, the person is turned off, and they step out of your life.

Here is a solution. You put the choice onto the table in front of the person. You ask, "So, I'm wondering which way you are leaning—towards investing in our project or being an advisor?"

3. Invite them to share their take

It can help when you ask, "I'm wondering what your take is on the _____ section?" People like to be asked for their opinion.

On the other hand, avoid using the words, "What's your opinion?" The word "opinion" sounds like it's something soft and not built on solid fact. Several people think that there is a disconnect between "opinion" and reality.

However, to ask for someone's *take* means you're looking for their understanding, which is likely based on their experience and wisdom.

With my clients, I talk about structure. That is, we can use the structure of language to set people at ease and to get them to lean in our direction. When you say, "I'm wondering what your take on this is....?"—you are demonstrating that you respect the investor's approach, intelligence and insights. A classic phrase is: *"If you go into a meeting asking for money, you'll get advice. If you ask for advice, you'll get money."*

4. Focus on "Forgive Me"

If you're ready to recover from sounding like you're pushing, you can feel at ease. Of course, investors expect you to be enthusiastic and passionate about your offering. However, you may cross a line during the conversation. You can use this *Recovery Method:* Say something like: "Forgive me. I got so excited about the XY part. How about we backtrack a couple steps?"

5. Target "what is working for you?"

When you work with an investor, you still want to come across as a peer. You might be deeply in debt, and they might have a hundred million dollars. But for the investor to be talking to you, the investor is revealing something. They have an interest because you might be *the one*. Realize that you have more power than you might think. You hold the prize—that is, you have the idea, and you have the courage and team. You're going forward, and you have the resolve.

So, be forthright and comfortable as you ask, "I'm curious. What is working for you about ____?"

6. Nurture and pivot on "I'm curious"

If your pitch falls into an awkward moment, nurture yourself and the developing relationship with the investor. How? Say, "I'm curious. What do you think is most important about ____?"

7. Open a story

At any time, you find yourself in an awkward moment,

you can launch a story. You can say, "This reminds me of the time when I learned …"

8. Work in the mutual friend

If something is not working in the conversation, you can get yourself and the investor to a comfortable energy by referring to a detail that relates to your mutual connection. You could say something like: "I remember that Sarah mentioned that you thought the ____ was important."

This process is valuable because you are associating the positive feeling that the investor has for your mutual friend with your currently developing conversation and relationship.

Power Principle: Rehearse ways to shift out of awkward moments and develop the investor's trust in you.

Power Question: With whom will you practice the following methods?

S – set their permission
H – hear their leaning this way or that
I – invite them to share their take
F – focus on "forgive me"
T – target "what is working for you?"
N – nurture and pivot on "I'm curious"
O – open a story
W – work in the mutual friend

Section Six

How can I experience real confidence and gain the trust of investors? (Secrets of *Extreme Confidence*—and featuring the *Confidence Toolkit Blueprint*)

Countermeasure: Develop Extreme Confidence as you use the Confidence Toolkit Blueprint.

What's the fastest way for you to gain the confidence of the investor? It's for you to come across as genuine and truly confident in yourself and your startup business.

Over a span of years, I developed something I call *Extreme Confidence.* This is a process in which you know deeply that you can perform at your best in the toughest moments. Here I'll give a brief and to-the-point overview of some essential elements of Extreme Confidence.

We begin with the **3 A's of Extreme Confidence**

- Above confidence in the text
- Adapt (*Recovery Methods*)
- Align the space with the audience

1. Above confidence in text
Many of us can memorize the words of a text and still feel

significant fear. Why? Because we're afraid that our mind will go blank. It happens.

After more than two decades of being a professional speaker, I do not fear moments of going blank. How? It's because I've developed material, I call *Recovery Methods*, which keep me in a *posture of poise.* Then I get back on track.

Additionally, I help clients do what I call, *Directed Rehearsal.* In another part of this book, I talk about the difference between *Directed Rehearsal* and *Default Rehearsal.*

Default Rehearsal is connected to rumination over details that you fear. Research demonstrates that under stress, human beings fall back on their default setting.

All of us fall into Default Rehearsal. The solution is *Directed Rehearsal.*

Directed Rehearsal includes practicing your Recovery Methods (which I'll discuss in the next section).

My point here is **confidence in the text is *not* enough.** You need to have confidence in your ability to adapt and flow with anything that may arise in the crucial pitch before an audience of investors or the crucial one-on-one meeting. Remember, the investor seeks to protect himself or herself by asking you the hard questions. To have Extreme Confidence you need to identify the 10 Worst Questions. Then you think through and prepare 3 answers for each of the 10 Worst Questions. You'll be more prepared then many people who attempt to perform at their best with investors.

2. Adapt (*Recovery Methods*)

How can you adapt if you mind goes blank? I already covered methods to handle that situation in a previous section.

The essential point about Recovery Methods is that you need to customize them *to yourself.*

For example, you could say, "I need to pause a moment. I want my response to be valuable to you." However, you don't know if this phrase works coming out of your mouth—until you try it.

Try it now. Say it aloud.

Did it work for you?

If not, how about this version: "I'm going to pause. I want to get to something that's meaningful."

Another way to buy yourself some time is this comment: "I see the value of your question. I haven't looked at it quite that way before. I'll take a moment. I want my response to be valuable for you."

Why does this process work?

It's because on average, our brains work at 700 words per minute. So, as you say your memorized line, your brain can find the answers you next want to express.

Keep a Progress Log of the session you have (even just 9 minutes) of saying your Recovery Words out loud. Then you will prove to yourself that you can adapt. You have evidence that you're preparing well. I call this *Behavior Change Through Incremental Evidence.*

3. Align the space with the audience

Confident people know how to use their body language to communicate, *I am trustworthy.*

 If you're addressing a room full of investors and one asks you a tough question, you avoid the amateur mistake of taking a few steps backward.

Your mouth could be saying, *"I'm confident that our product can solve that situation."* But if you are walking a couple steps backwards, you look like you're afraid of the question. Additionally, you look like you're afraid of that particular investor.

It takes practice to walk toward the question. That's the reason that I have participants in my workshop, *Convince Investors to Fund You,* rehearse within their small groups.

You practice walking toward the investor who asked the question and say a phrase like, "George, I see that's important to you." This builds rapport with the investor.

Often someone, who is on the edge of investing, will ask you tough questions because they want to be sure that they're making the right decision.

So, you need to align this space between you and the investor.

It helps to mention the person's name. If you don't know the person's name you can say, "I can see that's important to you. Oh, as you know, I'm [your first name], and you are?"

Confidence Toolkit Blueprint

To create real confidence, you do well to take effective action. Here's what you get in the below *Confidence Toolkit Blueprint*

- Proven Methods to improve your skills so that you *know* that you'll feel confident in a tough situation
- Reliable ways to improve how you prepare for any media appearance (videos for your YouTube channel, appearances on others' podcasts and more)
- Truly empowering methods for you to effectively face risk and seize opportunities to be successful

We'll use the P.O.W.E.R.S. process:

P – place a 9-minute Rehearsal in the morning
O – open with a 2-minute Rehearsal with a friend
W – work on audio recordings ("showtime")
E – engage Incremental Evidence
R – realize Recovery Methods
S – Set *Better Than Zero* (Progress Log)

1. Place a 9-minute Rehearsal in the morning

To make sure that you get the most from your rehearsal, place it in the morning. Your subconscious mind will work on your speech or project all day long. You can use lateral thinking, which occurs as your subconscious mind works on a project, while your conscious mind works on something else. Some of your best creativity will rise from your subconscious mind while you're taking a walk, for example.

2. Open with a 2-minute Rehearsal with a friend

When we're creating, we need support, but we must be careful of not leaning too much on friends. So, break down your project. Develop a circle of friends whom you help and who will help you. Still, be sure to ask them for 2 minutes of their time. Be sure to use a timer and make certain to avoid overstaying your welcome. Then your friends will not dread your phone call. Additionally, they get to enjoy helping you. Be sure to help them in return.

3. Work on audio recordings ("showtime")

I often have my clients include audio recording of their material. I've taught MBA students public speaking, and it was *not* my practice to use video in the beginning of that class. Why? We *avoid* someone becoming too self-conscious of how they move their elbow or how they tilt their head. That makes a person become stiff in their delivery. However, when you turn on an audio recorder, *it's showtime.* That's great because we want to have your adrenaline going—and have you feel that *this is important.* Using an audio recorder creates urgency and serves powerfully—rather than merely speaking to a wall.

4. Engage Incremental Evidence

When I say engage *incremental evidence,* I'm referring to a major, foundational part of *Extreme Confidence.* You are truly confident because you have witnessed your actual improvements. I have clients practice using Recovery Methods, so they become comfortable in answering tough questions. Reading a book, without actual practice taking tough questions, fails to give the incremental evidence that helps you experience real confidence.

5. Realize Recovery Methods

When I have taught MBA students public speaking, including at Stanford University, I begin with *Recovery Methods.* The reason for rehearsing Recovery Methods is that you quiet down fear.

For example, at IBM while giving a speech, I got stuck. So, I said, "I need to pause for a moment. My brain needs more RAM." At IBM, they found that comment to be hilarious. Better than that, I came across with poise.

The vital process is to pick your Recovery Methods and then rehearse them with as much diligence as you rehearse the content of your speech.

Here are examples of Recovery Methods:
You can say:
- I need to pause for a moment. I want my response to be valuable to you.
- At this moment, I want to emphasize …

The second method above helps if your mind gets stuck. You can emphasize anything that you said earlier in your speech.

Recovery Methods help you demonstrate your poise.

Here is a related method that I call **Walk and Plant.** Walk to a side of the audience and then stand in that spot. In this way you dispel some nervous energy, and you avoid looking nervous with needless pacing. In essence, you walk and then plant your feet.

6. Set *Better Than Zero* (Progress Log)

How can you make sure that you feel that you're prepared to give a speech or make a media appearance?

How can you expand your real confidence?

You log your rehearsals. Even if you just rehearse for 9 minutes a day over two weeks, you have written evidence that you have been rehearsing.

Some may say that 9 minutes is not much. However, 9 minutes each day is **Better than Zero.** And, for each daily 9-minute rehearsal session, your subconscious mind works on the material. Log your rehearsals in a Progress Log.

Often, I complete a daily rehearsal just for the good feeling of noting in my Progress Log that I completed this action.

When you make incremental progress on a daily basis, you feel proud of yourself. You feel good that you are rising to a higher level of creativity and skill. This is part of a process I call *Behavior Change through Incremental Evidence.*

Remember, you can develop real confidence when you use the tools in this *Confidence Toolkit Blueprint.*

P – place 9-minute Rehearsal in the morning

O – open with a 2-minute Rehearsal with a friend

W – work on audio recording ("showtime")

E – engage Incremental Evidence

R – realize Recovery Methods

S – Set *Better Than Zero* (Progress Log)

Develop Your Extreme Confidence: Use the *Intrigue Point* and the *Cool Factor*

For years in guiding MBA students and Master's Degree students (in fields like Communication, E-commerce, Web Design), I've emphasized that **any story needs** *The Cool Factor.* That's the moment when the person leans in and says, "This is cool!" We've seen early moments in feature films when the audience locks in with the perception—"This movie is going to be cool."

Working with clients who seek funding for their startup businesses, I've brought the understanding of The Cool Factor—plus something I call *The Intrigue Point* into play.

For example, when working with clients who meet new people at an event, and then want to guide the new people to a specific demonstration, I send an email with material like this:

"1. What is the "Intrigue Point" to get people to show up for your demonstration?

The Intrigue Point relates to phrasing your invitation, so the person is captivated, and their curiosity compels them to attend.

The Intrigue Point **example:**

"We're been in stealth mode. This is the debut for a select group of people, like you—of a revolution in _____.

This solves the problem in ____.

You do *not* want to miss it. You'll want to see this."

2. What is the "The Cool Factor" to get people to attend your demonstration?

The Cool Factor actually has an element of "this will be fun"—"this will be something to talk about." Being able to talk about some cool and innovative forms a type of incentive for people to attend. It's great to be *in the know.*

The Cool Factor **example:**

"It's the Cool Solution to ____."

"It's a delightful surprise to ____."

You can hand out a small card that reads: *VIP invitation — Secret Debut for a Select Group. By invitation only."*

3. How will you "close the sale" to be sure that people will show up like they say they will?

Just because someone says, "Yes, I'll attend your demonstration" does *not* mean they will go to your booth or to the meeting room you have in the same building.

You need to "close the sale." I'd rather say, "Set the agreement." People live up to agreements. Even a simple interchange of "So, I can count on seeing you there in 30 minutes?" "Yes"—will get you more people in the seats. You gave them an agreement to live up to. And, they agreed.

4. Have fun with it.

Let's say someone gives you some resistance about attending a meeting with lunch provided. They might say, "So what's in it for me?"

"You mean in addition to the free lunch?" you say, while giving them a big smile. You demonstrate that you're *not* uncomfortable at all with their teasing you.

People who are confident in the value they bring, do *not* sweat the small stuff. They look unruffled. They're having a good time, and others often want to bask in that radiating energy of confidence and good cheer.

Taylor Cone encourages us to begin with empathy which will empower our pitch and connection with investors.

Interview with Taylor Cone

1) What is crucial for someone pitching to do?

Any time you're addressing an audience (even an audience of one), your message will be more impactful and effective if you start from a place of empathy. Just like designers begin by attempting to understand their user's perspective and needs, you must understand who your audience is (background, experience, expertise), what they care about and why, and even how they're showing up that day. It could be as simple as knowing how to pronounce their name, a mistake Nike infamously made in their 2013 pitch to NBA superstar Stephen Curry, or as significant as ignoring their background, which Reebok did when they lost Beyoncé's athleisure line, failing to include anyone on the team who, in Beyoncé's words, "reflects my background, my skin color, and where I'm from and what I wanna do."

Take extreme ownership not just of your intent, but of your impact. When you do, you'll create a strong, trusting connection between you and your audience.

2) What mistake does the pitch-maker need to avoid?

Never have your pitch be the first time you do your pitch. In the design world, prototyping is everything. Prototyping your pitch allows you to practice, enables you to learn (from hearing yourself as well as feedback from others), and identifies any gaps that might exist. It's also a good idea to prototype a Q&A session—what questions should you expect and be prepared to answer? That way, when the time comes for your pitch, it's like riding a bike.

3) Knowing what you know now, what would you have done differently in business?

I would have been more fearless. Very few things in the world are truly irreparable or unresolvable, and realizing this is an empowering thought. I would have tried more things and more completely committed to the "forgiveness not permission" philosophy. Similarly, embracing a "good enough is better than perfect" approach unblocks me regularly. Publish that blog post you don't think is quite ready. Put that prototype that you're not quite sure is finished in front of someone for feedback. Schedule that event you don't think you have quite enough time to organize. You might be shocked at how much of success is simply about putting things in motion. Take that first step.

Taylor Cone helps people work better together. He believes in the power of creative collaboration to enable teams to do amazing things. He is the Founder & CEO of Lightshed, an innovation, leadership, and design firm that specializes in facilitation and executive coaching. Taylor has worked in the U.S. and internationally with clients including Fortune 500 companies, city governments, startups, non-profits, and foundations. Taylor is a Certified Professional Coach through the Institute for Professional Excellence in Coaching (iPEC), where he also holds an Energy Leadership Index Master Practitioner certification. A former Lecturer and current coach at the Stanford d.school, he's taught courses including Design Thinking Bootcamp and Design for Extreme Affordability. Taylor is also a Board Member and river guide for ARTA River Trips, a non-profit rafting company. Whether on the river or in the office, Taylor's passion is for guiding individuals and teams through transformative experiences. www.lightshed.co

Power Principle: Develop Extreme Confidence as you use the Confidence Toolkit Blueprint.

Power Questions: When will you being rehearsing Recovery Methods? Who is someone you trust and who will listen you as you rehearse? Will you work with a coach?*

* Reach Tom Marcoux at GetTheBigYES.com

Section Seven

How can I speak with No Fear?

Countermeasure: Correct a *Default Rehearsal* with a *Directed Rehearsal.*

Where does the fear come from? For many of us, on some level, we feel we're *not* ready. How can we feel ready?

We learn to shift from Default Rehearsal to Directed Rehearsal.

- *Default Rehearsal* – This includes rumination over past mistakes. It also includes fearful projection as to what might go wrong. Some people merely "rehearse in their head."
- *Directed Rehearsal* – You practice Recovery Methods, and you rehearse with the guidance of a coach.* Rehearsing aloud helps you fine tune your *instrument* (vocal tonality, posture, word choice, body language).

* I coach clients via Skype and in person in my work as Spoken Word Strategist and Executive Coach.

We'll use the A.I.M process.
A – ask compelling questions (30 answers)
I – imagine best outcomes
M – measure

1. Ask compelling questions (30 answers)

What are the *10 Worst Questions the investor can ask*? This is a *compelling question* that can launch you into excellent Directed Rehearsal.

What would you rehearse? You would rehearse three good answers that you could use to respond to one of the Worst Questions.

Ultimately, you think through and prepare a total of 30 responses (three for each of the 10 Worst Questions.)

Here are two more compelling questions:

- What is most important to an investor who would invest in your startup business?
- How can you demonstrate traction to this investor?

2. Imagine best outcomes

To hit a target, you must see the target. We do this by imagining best outcomes. In order to get an investor to fund your startup business, you need to design your pitch, so all elements inevitably lead to a big YES. (By the way, my website is GetTheBigYES.com).

I ask my client: "So, tell me. How do you see the investor saying YES? What is the crucial detail that gets them to smile and say, 'Okay. I'm in'?"

3. Measure

How do you know you're getting better? You measure your rehearsals. You keep track of how many sessions and how much time you put in.

I even use a Progress Log as I type these words. I know at this moment that this book is 38,549 words. I also know that I typed 1,019 words today.

Use a Progress Log so that you can prove to yourself that

you are doing the required preparation to perform at your best.

Additionally, measure the time you practice your Recovery Methods. (See another section of this book for Recovery Methods that you can use if your mind goes blank—during a pitch).

In summary, you eliminate fear by taking conscious and deliberate action toward preparing to perform at your best. No wise stage actor would get on stage without enough excellent rehearsal.

Similarly, we use the A.I.M. process to hone our craft— that is, we are professional in our approach to pitching.

Power Principle: Correct a *Default Rehearsal* with a *Directed Rehearsal.*

Power Question: When will you rehearse? (Consider rehearsing for 9 minutes in the morning before your brush your teeth. In this way, your subconscious mind can work on the material all day.)

Tom Marcoux

Section Eight

How do I show confidence when under fire from an investor's tough question?

Countermeasure: Rehearse methods to gain time so you avoid looking scared and avoid burning a bridge to the investor.

When a tough question hits you as a bad surprise, you must avoid two things. First, avoid looking scared, and second, avoid blurting out some comment that will burn the bridge to the investor

We'll use the G.O. process:

G – gain time
O – offer a response in 2 days

1. Gain time

Your goal is to buy yourself some time so you can think before you offer an answer to a tough question.

Investors want thoughtful people. The investor may be *testing* to see if you're thoughtful, deliberate and careful with your words.

You can respond with one of these comments:
- I see that's important to you …
- I need to pause for a moment. I want my response to be valuable to you …

Try those comments out. Say them aloud. Then see what phrase works for you. Perhaps, you'll customize some phrase that helps you get a few critical seconds to think. I call this getting some *thinkspace*.

2. Offer a response in 2 days

If an investor asks you a question and you do not have a definitive answer, is it okay to "fake it"? **No!**

Why?

The reason is that if you fake it and you're caught, you've lost the whole game.

Instead, we need you to respond firmly and with confidence, "I'll look into that, and I expect I can get you an answer on Thursday afternoon. How does that sound?"

In this example I am identifying a time and date that **are 2 days after the conversation**. Why? Because we don't know what's going to happen that evening or the next morning.

Perhaps, one might face a family emergency or an emergency at work. If you promise too much, like *I'll get that to you tomorrow morning* but find yourself staying up all night tending to the health needs of a family member, you might miss this important deadline. Instead, buy yourself time.

In summary, make sure that you use the methods of G.O.—so that you avoid the two big mistakes of looking scared or burning a bridge to the investor.

Instead, you'll come across as confident and professional.

* * * * * *

I'll now share my interview with David Joud who gives us insights in how you need allies to be present in a room when you pitch ...

Interview with David Joud

1) What is crucial for someone pitching to do?

Many startup founders make the critical mistake of being too technical. It is crucial that a person makes a pitch with an emotional appeal. In my experience judging a number of pitches, I have found that startup founders need to make an emotional connection with investors. The investors need to know the vision of the startup founders. If you don't engage my emotions, and I don't know exactly what you are trying to accomplish to benefit customers, then we have a non-starter.

To make this emotional connection with the audience, founders need to pay attention to three critical factors. First and foremost, they need to protect their intellectual property by patenting their ideas, processes and products. This ensures that they can have some level of discussion where they can gain favorable attention when they are discussing their ideas. This involves some legal work, well worth the investment (which always ends up increasing the value of their startup).

Then, they must make friends: Networking with investors and making friends before the pitch is critical. Having those networking discussions and discovering what investors are looking for will help the founders tailor their pitch and get valuable input on their ideas. Lastly, having a strong vision that others want to get behind will win investors over before the pitch.

This work is critical and takes time. When they craft a vision statement that is both short and powerful, they will win over the crowd and may not even have to pitch to get investors' interest and support. The well-crafted vision statement wins everyone over and generates a stronger emotional connection with investors!

Tom: What mistake does the pitch-maker need to avoid?

David: A major mistake that startup founders fall into is staying in stealth mode too long. When startup founders pitch, they really need to have a network and to have allies in the audience. These allies will talk up the value of the startup company.

Additionally, one needs to emphasize values within your startup company. For example, I was working with a client and the founders of the company were talking about creating great revenue, but they were missing the powerful vision that would engage investors. During my coaching, my client's whole energy changed when they identified that their true value was to "end world hunger." That is a vision that intrigues an audience of investors. That is a vision that can be fundable.

Tom: Knowing what you know now, what would you have done differently?

David: I would have gone into coaching much sooner. For years, I had a truly successful consulting company. I wrote many powerful reports that had good ideas in them. Only a very small portion of the good ideas were implemented. However, in coaching, I support the company leaders to come up with their own good ideas. They have ownership over these ideas, and so they implement them. I also help companies that have multiple partners in leadership. I help them connect on a common ground of values. I help them reconnect with a passion and vision that they started the company with. Coaching is such a successful paradigm because it is more reliable for people to implement their own ideas, while being supported.

David Joud, President of Dynamic Strategic Alignment, is a Certified Business Coach who speaks regularly at events and interactive workshops. He works primarily with top level executives and entrepreneurs. His seminars and speaking subjects are presented in an interactive setting. Participants always gain great insight they can use immediately, and we share the feedback we received with the event organizer. www.dsalignment.com

Power Principle: Rehearse methods to gain time so you avoid looking scared and avoid burning a bridge to the investor.

Power Questions: What responses will you use to gain time—if an investor asks you a tough question? Who will support you and listen as you rehearse for facing a tough question with poise and confidence?

Reminder:
Get Access to Free Videos to Take Your Skills to a Higher Level
Go to GetTheBigYES.com/YourAdvantage

Section Nine

What can I do if I lose heart in my project/company?

Countermeasure: Use the *3 R's of Empowering Your Heart.*

One of my clients said, "I just found out that investors in the USA do not invest in my kind of company."

When I hear a client say something like that, I invite them to pause for a moment. Whatever information they just saw that says that investors in the USA don't invest in X-type of company—*this is just one datapoint.* Additionally, you only need *one investor* to open the door for other investors. So, we notice getting disheartened by one piece of news can be crippling and unnecessary.

Still, this is a real phenomenon—becoming disheartened by one piece of news. Then, add all the rejection experiences one gets on the fundraising trail, and it's important that you have methods to help you climb out of an emotional rut.

We'll use the *3 R's of Empowering Your Heart.*

- Realize that "it's just one datapoint"
- Return to the essence of your vision
- Revitalize by "Changing on a Dime" … Adapt

1. Realize that "it's just one datapoint"
I've already mentioned two vital elements

a) It's just one datapoint
b) You only need one investor to get started

Here, we'll add: "It is just one datapoint. We don't really know what it means."

We might have a guess that some "expert" has noticed a trend that USA investors avoid X-type of company. However, just one investor might change their mind. Or you might be bringing something so extraordinary that an investor can experience an Aha Moment or a Moment of Discovery. That's the time when you can convince an investor to fund you.

The point here is: Do *not* let one datapoint stop you in your tracks. The metaphor could be: "Oh. It's raining. I'll bring an umbrella." You still leave for your business meeting.

2. Return to the essence of your vision

Why did you start your company in the first place? What was your vision? What made your heart beat faster? What great benefit were you bringing to your future customers/clients?

We get so bogged down in fundraising details that we can forget the whole point of our endeavor. Sure, you can say, "Our company disrupts the XY industry. We're the first to help people do ____." Unfortunately, many people start to tune out to their own message due to the human experience of familiarity dulls our senses.

Pause. Remember when you first burst with energy as you told someone you trusted about your Great New Idea.

Additionally, one of my mentors said that people who sell something get disheartened by focusing on the wrong people.

He set up these categories:
- Top 2% (are completely in sync with your vision)
- Middle 20%
- Bottom 20% (will never invest)

"Where do you think people concentrate their efforts?" he asked.

"I would hope that they'd focus on the Top 2%," I replied.

"Many of them use up their time on the Middle 20%" he said.

My point here is to encourage you to focus on the Top 2% and your original vision. *Reconnect and reenergize yourself.*

3. Revitalize by "Changing on a Dime" … Adapt

The great thing about running your own business is that you can adapt and change. An old phrase is *stop on a dime*. This means to stop quickly on such a small coin.

The truth is: You can stop on a dime and create a change fast.

It's reported that FedEx began as an idea related to banking. However, Fred Smith found it necessary to change course to a delivery service we see today.

Similarly, when Steve Jobs returned to Apple, he promptly changed course and cancelled many good projects in favor of focusing on extraordinary projects.

"You think, well, focusing is saying yes. No, focusing is about saying no. … I'm as proud of many of the things we haven't done as the things we have done. Innovation is saying no to a thousand things."– Steve Jobs

"You should never start a company with the goal of getting rich. Your goal should be making something you believe in and

making a company that will last." – Steve Jobs

At times, I invite a client to look at the whole industry. I ask, "Can you up-level this?" By this I mean, can your original idea transform to a higher level of service?

You can stop on a dime and adapt. In doing this, you can empower and uplift your heart.

Power Principle: Use the *3 R's of Empowering Your Heart.*

Power questions: Can you up-level what service/product your company delivers? Can you up-level your ideas? Will you quiet down fear that one datapoint may intensify? What are your other options?

Section Ten

How can I stay strong and keep going forward in the face of Rejection Trouble?

Countermeasure: Examine the responses you get, change your language and reduce the number of No's you receive.

When I speak on "Secrets for Your Courage and Freedom from Rejection Trouble," I share strategies to empower the audience to stay strong in the face of rejection.

Many times, when something seems like a rejection, it's actually the person melting down next to you. This happens a lot in life because we're all impacted with too much to do. I don't call this rejection; I rename it as "no match."

When I say *freedom from rejection trouble,* I don't mean that you're going to reframe everything as not being rejection. You can be going through a tough time when you're not getting a number of *Yes's.*

In this section, we cover ways to reduce the number of No's.

Rejection trouble is really when rejection can paralyze you.

Instead, we'll use the R.E.F. process. Basically, you are the referee—the one who calls something "in" or "out." You make the distinctions that can empower you.

R - reframe to "no match" and "Next!"

E - examine, predict, reduce *No's*

F - focus

1. Reframe to "no match" and "Next!"

I've encouraged my clients and audiences with a certain phrase:

If you have one and you lose one, it's a tragedy.
If you have 20 and you lose one, it's just a step.

By this I mean, if you have 20 prospective investors, and you lose one of them, you don't melt down.

Realize that even some of the most likely investors will not invest for their reasons. And, these reasons can be arbitrary or even temporary.

Earlier I mentioned that a person may not be rejecting you or your startup business. That person may be melting down next to you. How are they melting? Perhaps, they're going through a divorce, or their daughter is dealing with teenage-pregnancy, or they have a cold.

So that was not a rejection, that was "no match." (At least, it was a "no match" at the time.)

Still, realize that some people will simply not invest ... ever. See the signs and move on. How? Tell yourself, "Next!"—encouraging yourself to find other prospective investors.

2. Examine, predict, reduce "No's"

During my workshop, *Convince Investors to Fund You*, I reveal that investors often say, "Where's your traction?" They're looking for positive answers to questions like:

- What have you proved?
- Do people actually want this thing you're talking

about?

- Have you tested it?
- Has there been a focus group?
- Is there any data that backs up that what you're doing is viable now?

If you keep getting the same question as "what's your traction", you must *examine it*. You can *predict* how you will answer it. After you have watched people's responses to your answer, you can predict, to some degree, what works.

This helps you *reduce the number of No's* you face.

Reducing the number of No's helps you *get more Yeses*.

And this strengthens you to face the next round of No's.

You want to augment everything that works towards the *Yes*, and you want to eliminate the distractions that create "no."

As you examine what is working or not working for your pitch, realize that you need to get an *Immediate Yes* response inside the investor.

What does that mean? It means, at least subconsciously, the investor is thinking: "Hmm. Looks interesting. This person seems reliable. I'll listen—at least for the next 10 minutes."

Why do you need that Immediate Yes response? Researchers have noticed something called **"thin slicing"— that's when someone makes a quick decision based on a thin bit of information.** They decide quickly in terms of: "Am I in or am I out?"

You want to make sure that you begin a pitch with material that guides the investor to the Immediate Yes. They will keep watching to see if something changes their mind and their immediate assessment. Make sure you remove distractions that can turn the Yes-assessment into a No.

Keep examining the responses you get and keep refining your material.

3. Focus

In speeches and with clients, I frequently talk about *The Power of Three.*

If you're feeling overwhelmed because you're focused on having 20 prospects, you can use the Power of Three. How? Focus on the Top Three Most Likely People to invest in your startup business.

I ask my clients, "Who are the top three most likely people who will say *yes* to you?"

Focus is essential.

"People think focus means saying yes to the thing you've got to focus on. But that's not what it means at all. It means saying no to the hundred other good ideas that there are. You have to pick carefully. – Steve Jobs

Additionally, The Power of Three returns us to *examine, predict, and reduce No's.*

If you know that investors will raise certain points of concern (objections), you develop three responses to each point. Again, that's The Power of Three. You're feeling stronger because you have *three answers* to a particular point of concern.

By the way, I prefer to say *point of concern* because if an investor asks you a question it can be great step on the staircase of saying YES to you.

On a daily basis, use The Power of Three to focus on the Top Three Things you need to do *today*

In summary, use these methods:

R - reframe to "no match" and "Next!"

E - examine, predict, reduce *No's*

F - focus

When you use these methods, you will get *Yeses,* and that will raise your energy. That process will transform the idea of rejection into a quiet voice in the background. And, you will move forward faster.

Power Principle: Examine the responses you get, change your language and reduce the number of No's you receive.

Power Questions: What is the worst question an investor can ask you? How can you have a strong, credible response to the question, *where's your traction*?

Tom Marcoux

Part 2

Overcome the Deadly Mistakes

What stands between you and getting funding? The Deadly Mistakes.

They are the elements of a bad impression. That's when you're perceived with a number of these unfortunate characteristics:

- Unsure
- Unconfident
- Ignorant of vital details
- Uncoachable
- Inflexible
- Arrogant

What is the solution?

Drop what I call *Default Rehearsal* and replace it with Directed Rehearsal.

- *Default Rehearsal* is the ineffective automatic practice that includes rumination, practicing wrong actions, and fretting about potential future missteps and bad consequences.

- *Directed Rehearsal* is work you do with a coach, so you are adept with flowing with difficulties in the moment. You practice Recovery Methods, so you handle your mind going blank—while you maintain poise and confidence.

Where does real confidence come from? Evidence. I have a term I share with clients and audiences: *Behavior Change through Incremental Evidence.* By this I mean, you have kept a Progress Log of all your rehearsals, so you know you are making real progress in being fully prepared to excel during your pitch.

Here I'll go into brief material about how to deal with the Deadly Mistakes:

1. Unsure

Rehearse your 3 responses for each of 10 Worst Questions.

6. Unconfident

Practice powerful body language. Walk toward the question (and the investor) and say, "I see how important that is to you."

7. Ignorant of vital details

Study some material about your industry and the startup fundraising process every day. Work with knowledgeable and skilled mentors. Hire an Executive Coach. (You can reach me through GetTheBigYES.com)

8. Uncoachable

Rehearse a personal story that reveals how you took the advice of a mentor and gained excellent results.

9. Inflexible

Rehearse a story that demonstrates how you were flexible and responsive to a tough situation—and gained a triumphant result.

10. Arrogant

Be sure to share stories that demonstrate how you are coachable and flexible. Realize that people cannot trust someone who never admits a mistake. Their impression is that the person cannot grow and improve because they cannot see shortcomings—and areas that need improvement.

Demonstrate how you have identified areas to improve and how your purposely sought coaching to increase your skills.

Power Principle: Devote conscious and deliberate action to overcome the Deadly Mistakes.

Power Questions: As you read the above Deadly Mistakes, what resonated with you? In what areas do you need to get coaching, so you're stronger and more skilled?

Reminder:
Get Access to Free Videos to Take Your Skills to a Higher Level
Go to GetTheBigYES.com/YourAdvantage

Tom Marcoux

Part 3

The C.O.M.P.E.L. process of
Compelling Brand Innovation

"So, you're going to tell me what works to get investors to fund my startup business," Amy, a new client, asked.

"Together, we're going to uncover what works for *you*," I replied, serving in my roles as Spoken Word Strategist and Executive Coach.

Over a span of years, I developed a system that I call *Compelling Brand Innovation.*

While working with a client, I ask the right questions and provide the empowering direction (like directing a stage or film performance). My process includes what I call *Directed Rehearsal*—which I discuss in several sections in this book.

For decades, I have pulled the Best Performance out of CEOs, podcast hosts, actors, speakers, small business leaders and more.

Compelling Brand Innovation is a process of digging to find what's in the heart of the client. We discover how best to use the client's "instrument" (voice, body language, word choice, values, goals, Natural Charm Charisma and Warm Trust Charisma). It's a process of discovery and revelation.

Here, we'll discuss the C.O.M.P.E.L. process:

C – conquer the noise
O – open the imagination

P – pinpoint with Engaging Language

E – engage innovation

L – light up a question

1. Conquer the noise

Your Compelling Brand cuts through the noise.

What noise? More than 5,000 ads per day (the number 5,000 was noted back in 2007, by the marketing firm Yankelovich, Inc.). Many researchers suggest we're inundated with more advertising messages now.

With so much noise, some researchers suggest that our default status is *distracted.* So many individuals complain that people, on social media, jump to conclusions. One of my friends writes a lot of commentary in social media. When someone pushes back, he'll write "Did you read my whole post?"

The truth is: Many of us do *not* read the whole post. Or if we make such an attempt, we're still facing distraction in our own thoughts.

So, what is the solution? Use **Engaging Language.** That's language that seizes attention and moves emotions.

As I address an audience, I often say, "I can move your thoughts and feelings with just two words."

Then I pause. Finally, I say, "Best friend."

If you have a good relationship at this moment with a best friend, you might feel a warm, full feeling in your heart area.

If a friend betrayed you, you might feel *something else.* If you don't feel you have a best friend—a chasm of loneliness may open.

Catch that word choice of *chasm of loneliness?* It's evocative.

Word choice is also vital in terms of grabbing feelings as opposed to just conveying an intellectual idea. Note the difference in feeling that words evoke: "gave it another attempt" versus *"risked everything in one last try."*

Sometimes, words come with so much baggage that it's best that we don't use those certain words. We do better to revise our phrases.

Remember your compelling brand cuts through the noise. With so much competition for any part of the mindshare of the consumer or potential high-level colleagues or investors, you need to express the most compelling elements of your brand in a *brief manner*. Here's an example. On my business card, I use just four words to describe a strong element of what I do: "Right Words ==> More Clients."

Now I invite you to answer this question for yourself: How can you design what you say to be brief and compelling?

2. Open the imagination

You can access the imagination with an image, an idea or words. Here are five words that can lead you to a real feeling: *most important person to you*. That phrase might bring up the face of your romantic partner.

Sometimes, we use a *question* to get access to someone's imagination. When addressing a class of MBA students, I pointed out the difference between saying, "Women live longer than men" versus **"*Why* do women live longer than men?"**

When working with a client, I share this phrase: "Image – Question – Story."

Here's an example of an image (as revealed by few words): "Rearranging the chairs on the Titanic." This is the epitome of a useless effort.

Here are possible questions:

- How would your life be if you could get_____ out of the way?
- If you were able to double your sales in 27 days, how much better would your life be? How would that feel?

Imagine hearing a brief story:

"It's 10:15—on Monday night. Sarah closes the front door behind her. She hears a strange and bad sound from the living room. Her heart pounds in her chest. Could this be the horrible—".

A brief story does capture attention—yes?

3. Pinpoint with Engaging Language.

The best brand names don't describe. They stand for a big idea-- [one] that translates into emotional appeal. Nike is about winning. GoPro is about heroism. Apple is about simplicity and usability.
— Jonathan Bell

Okay, just a moment. Some people in my circle would say Apple is about cool gear that makes life so much better. And by the way, you look cool and sophisticated using Apple products. You're in the Apple circle.

My point here is that we want to choose our words carefully.

Make sure your words are evocative.

Provoke emotion.

How's that for two powerful words?

Unfortunately, I have seen rough drafts (pitches/slide decks) from highly intelligent clients that overemphasize merely logic, graphs, and a cerebral approach.

On the other hand, I guide my clients through the next iterations.

I ask questions including:

- What are the Best Results Your Clients (Investors) Want?
- What big benefit will your client *enjoy* when they use ____?
- What do they want to feel?

Clients can answer that the client (or investor) wants to feel ...

- Smart
- Better than others
- Safe
- Special—as part of an elite group

In speeches and workshops, I use Engaging Language.

When it comes to Engaging Language, I emphasize three things:

a) *Guide the audience's thoughts*

As the Spoken Word Strategist, I use my over two decades of experience in giving speeches to audiences. In my speeches, I carefully observe the facial expressions and body language of audience members. I note what they respond to.

I even lead the audience to think different thoughts when I say: "Oh, I see many of you nodding. I see you're right with me."

b) *Repeat the Detail 3 Times*

If you have an important point to make, don't try to be subtle or clever. Use a pile driver. Hit the point once. Then come back and

hit it again. Then hit it a third time — a tremendous whack.
– Winston Churchill

The powerful use of Engaging Language is when you identify something that's most important and you repeat it three times. Repeating something three times is a pattern I learned in screenwriting. When you want the audience to remember something, repeat the detail three times.

Remember Engaging Language is about cutting through the noise of everything out there that's competing for attention. Even when audience members look like they're listening, we do not have access to their internal monologue. Often, an audience member misses the chance to hear the first expression of an idea.

You can repeat a certain phrase three times so that by the end of your presentation, the audience members can *finish the sentence.* Here's an example:

"As we all can see, this new product saves time, saves money and disrupts the XY industry. Better thinking makes ...."

" —more profits," the audience finishes the sentence.

c) *Make an idea stick by developing a throughline and narrative.*

In my training as a screenwriter and feature film director I've learned how to develop the best in a narrative. A narrative must have a throughline, known as the "driving force of a story."

Here's an example of a story. Janet, a 17-year-old young woman tries out for a basketball team and fails.

However, a coaching assistant says, "There's something in you. I'll work with you at 6 a.m. every morning."

With dedication and perseverance, Janet makes the team

and becomes the star player. She sinks the winning basket at the same court where she had failed three times before.

In the above narrative, you even see the use of *bookends.* The first bookend is Janet's failing to make the team—at a particular court. The final bookend is sinking the winning basket at that same court.

You can adapt a narrative structure into a presentation or pitch.

4. Engage innovation

In my workshops *Convince Investors to Fund You* (that I've delivered in Silicon Valley California and in Thailand at the Igniters International Conference), I have emphasized what comprises a *big idea.*

A big idea that involves innovation includes unfair advantage, disruption, and big profits.

Innovation is often about combining things that exist. Or it is using a form of new technology in a new way—for example Uber and Lyft.

You can find relevant innovation opportunities when you ask questions like:

- How can we make this more convenient and faster to complete?
- Where is the real pain point for the user?
- Where do people feel frustration?

Frustration is a vital area to focus on. In research studies, people rate a phone call by the level of frustration they felt in previous phone calls that failed to resolve the problem. In a way, it doesn't matter if the fourth phone call is productive and truly courteous.

Years ago, I talked with three managers at a particular company until a fourth manager solved my problem in 40 seconds. The three previous phone calls and related frustration have a big impact on my impression of the company. Would I recommend that company? Would you?

My own company has this mission:
We create energizing, encouraging edutainment for our good and humankind's rise.

This leads to a question: How can we improve this and actually raise the level of benefit to humankind?

My point here is the *Catalyst for Innovation* is the use of excellent questions.

5. Light up a question.

How do you feel in hearing questions like:

What would you do if …?

How could you survive if …?

These questions remind me of the teaser moments that get people to watch broadcast news at 11 pm:

- "New virus crippling computers across the country. Your computer may be next.
- "Worse outbreak of ___ in fifty years. And local authorities are ignoring the consequences."

Earlier I mentioned the value of a question. When I say *light up a question,* I mean listen well and discover the question that will *fully engage* your listener. Focus on a question that aligns with their deepest concerns and their deepest desires.

One of the vital things I've learned as a storyteller, screenwriter and feature film director is: Have a strong a villain. To have a compelling brand and engage the listener, show how your product (or service) overcomes some horrible situation.

What or who could the villain could be?

- Local authorities who ignore dire consequences
- A complacent company that has left a backdoor to hackers
- Human ignorance

Sometimes, a client does well with talking up a bleak situation. Then, I say, "Don't leave the investors in the dark. Show how your innovative solution brightens the world."

I chose the words, *brightens the world,* with care. In fantasy stories, when something goes wrong, the entire land is blighted. In the animated feature film, *The Lion King,* when Scar, the villain, takes over as leader, all the food vanishes, and the sky and land go dark.

In summary, you do *not* want merely a "good brand." Instead, develop your Compelling Brand as you use the methods of the C.O.M.P.E.L. process. Provide two things clients (and investors) want—*hope and certainty.*

Power Principle: Make your brand compelling—provide hope and certainty.

Power Questions: What brief phrases engage your listener's emotions? How can you demonstrate that your solution brightens the client/investor's world?

Tom Marcoux

Part 4
New Material plus Classic Material from
Be Heard and Be Trusted
—celebrating 20 years

Twenty years ago, I developed material that became a book that I later retitled as *Be Heard and Be Trusted*. A version of that book went into the Cogswell Polytechnical College *Time Capsule* to be opened in 2100.

In subsequent years, I reformulated and refined the work. In celebration of my research and work with clients, MBA students (at Stanford University) and audiences, I'm sharing the below new material and classic material from *Be Heard and Be Trusted*. I'm also including new interviews with a billionaire, millionaires, a former deputy manager at NASA and more.

Be Heard-20 Method #1

Great Communicators Handle Fear

What if you could handle fear and get it out of your way? How amazing and fulfilling would your life be?

As you learn how to handle fear, you will become someone who is heard and trusted. Top professionals are heard and trusted because people believe that they can handle fear with grace and strength.

The greatest communicators have a special advantage: they are skilled in communicating with themselves. They talk to themselves in ways that get them into action.

How do you talk to yourself about your fears? Many people have become paralyzed by fear. If they have read some idea about how to deal with their fear, trying to apply that idea merely frustrates them.

Fear defeats more people than any other one thing in the world.
– Ralph Waldo Emerson

The good news is that this section will help you work with the fear and transform it into something you can use to lift your life to a higher level of success and fulfillment.

Courage is not the absence of fear, but rather the judgment that something else is more important than fear. – Meg Cabot

What could be more important than fear? Living your life with joy and fulfillment.

I don't believe people are looking for the meaning of life as much as they are looking for the experience of being alive.
– Joseph Campbell

Fear affects much of what we do and what we avoid doing. Some of us are truly diminished by the fear of being hurt. But if we have ways to deal with pain, we become stronger. We experience more freedom.

This discussion about fear is vital if you want to be a great communicator, someone who is heard and trusted. Great communicators deal with their own fears, and they help their audiences handle fear, too. Great communicators guide audiences to move beyond fear to real freedom.

To have the personal energy to handle fear, we often need to clear some emotional space. Here are Dr. Fred Luskin's comments on how to free ourselves from pain by engaging in the process of forgiveness.

Nine Steps of Forgiveness by Dr. Fred Luskin

My book *Forgive for Good: A Proven Prescription for Health and Happiness* is a primer on how to make peace when things you choose, or things chosen for you do not work out well. When painful things happen, you have a choice. I teach people to make more forgiving choices. I do this because I understand that as a function of life everyone will have painful experiences as well as pleasant ones. It is a singular power to be able to handle what comes your way without getting lost in blame and suffering. We do not know what the game of life has in store, but we do know that forgiveness is one way that provides strength to get back into the game.

As Director of the Stanford Forgiveness Projects my forgiveness methodology has been tested and shown to be successful through a number of research projects. We have demonstrated that forgiveness can reduce stress, blood pressure, anger, depression, hurt, and increase optimism, hope, compassion, physical vitality, and forgiveness. We have worked with people who have been lied to, cheated, abandoned, physically injured, beaten, abused or had their children murdered. Forgiveness training made a significant difference in many of their lives. What follows is our nine-step method of teaching and becoming forgiving.

Nine Steps to Forgiveness
1. Know exactly how you feel about what happened and

be able to articulate what about the situation is not OK. Then, tell a couple of trusted people about your experience.

2. Make a commitment to yourself to do what you have to do to feel better. Forgiveness is for you and not for anyone else.

3. Forgiveness does not necessarily mean reconciliation with the person that upset you or condoning of their action. What you are after is to find peace. Forgiveness can be defined as the "peace and understanding that come from blaming that which has hurt you less, taking the life experience less personally, and amending your grievance story."

4. Get the right perspective on what is happening. Recognize that your primary distress is coming from the hurt feelings, thoughts, and physical upset you are suffering now, not what offended you or hurt you two minutes—or ten years—ago.

5. At the moment you feel upset practice stress management to soothe your body's flight or fight response.

6. Give up expecting things from other people, or your life, that they do not choose to give you. Recognize the "unenforceable rules" you have for your health or how you or other people must behave. Remind yourself that you can hope for health, love, friendship and prosperity, and work hard to get them. However, you will suffer when you demand these things occur when you do not have the power to make them happen.

7. Put your energy into looking for another way to get your positive goals met than through the experience that has hurt you. I call this step finding your positive intention. Instead of mentally replaying your hurt, seek out new ways to get what you want.

8. Remember that a life well lived is your best revenge.

Instead of focusing on your wounded feelings, and thereby giving the person who caused you pain power over you, learn to look for the love, beauty, and kindness around you. Appreciate what you have more than attending to what you do not have.

9. Amend your grievance story to remind you of the heroic choice to forgive.

Dr. Fred Luskin, author of *Forgive for Good*, presents the forgiveness training methodology that has been validated through six successful research studies conducted through the Stanford Forgiveness Projects. His presentations explore the HEAL process of forgiveness that, when learned, can lead to enhanced well-being through self-care. In class practice may include guided imagery, journal writing and discussion all presented in a safe and nurturing environment. Dr. Luskin holds a Ph.D. in Counseling and Health Psychology from Stanford University.

Dr. Luskin continues to serve as Director of the Stanford Forgiveness Projects. In addition, his work has been successfully applied and researched in corporate, medical, legal and religious settings. He currently serves as a Senior Consultant in Health Promotion at Stanford University and is a Professor at the Institute of Transpersonal Psychology. He presents lectures, workshops, seminars and trainings on the importance, health benefits and training of forgiveness, stress management and emotional competence throughout the United States.

www.LearningToForgive.com

When we know how to deal with great pain, we can free up our personal energy. With more energy, we can take our lives and our businesses to higher levels.

The most successful people, those who enjoy personal fulfillment, are skillful in the ways they handle fear and disappointment. They realize this truth:

We fear the thing we want the most. – Dr. Robert Anthony

Some of us fear getting on a grander stage in life. Others fear more responsibilities that come with a higher-level role—like becoming CEO for the first time.

We can handle fear and greater responsibilities as we guard our personal energy.

* ** * * *

Be Heard-20 Method #2

Handle Criticism Well

The greatest communicators realize that fear subsides when you devote yourself to the process and focus in the moment.

The way you overcome shyness is to become so wrapped up in something that you forget to be afraid. – Lady Bird Johnson

The most productive people in any field realize that in order to improve, you need to practice your craft. We can also learn to deal with criticism of our earliest work. Some people feel social pressure because they fear that they cannot recover from the criticism of their early work.

I worked with a client, a filmmaker, who found that someone had taken excerpts from her first film and placed them on YouTube.com. She developed her own answers to criticism:

- "Did you laugh?"
- "Works for some; doesn't work for others."
- "That was at the beginning of my career."
- "That's a part of my body of work."

Just knowing how she would be able to respond to any criticism lowered my client's fear level. With less fear, she was free to devote her energy to her current work. Do you see how being prepared for criticism can free up your personal energy?

LaChelle Adkins shares insights in how being transparent actually sets other people at ease.

Interview with LaChelle Adkins

Tom: How can you develop more trust when you do *not* seek validation from others?

LaChelle: When you're *not* seeking validation, this process disarms people.

When you're able to accept your whole self, the good and bad, then this allows you to focus on the business at hand.

I'm not concerned about what happened to me yesterday—or even five minutes before I arrive at a business meeting. I am able to focus completely on what I'm doing. And I remember what it is that I'm there to bring to the table. I'm not looking for approval from other people.

I am at ease. I'm not judging myself harshly. I'm not judging the other people. Many people have seen my story about being hospitalized for stress as a weakness. And, I saw it that way for a long time. But then I realized that I had control in that outcome. I was no longer looking at it from a victim standpoint but now as a victor. Now, I can use that experience not only to help myself grow, but I can help others learn, who may be dealing with the same type of stresses, anxiety and depression that I had experienced.

You can be stronger when you don't seek validation. For example, if there was a car accident, and I arrive late to a meeting, I am not looking for other people to say, "It's okay that you're late." When I'm not looking for validation, I'm able to fill myself up with whatever I need to perform at my maximum potential—when I'm in the business meeting. To make this clearer: I recognize what I can control and what I cannot. So, in the case of arriving late to the meeting, I do *not* feel that others are judging me in a negative way. I feel the same about myself as if I arrived on time. This allows me to be stronger because I choose to be proactive rather than reactive about an accident that was out of my control.

Tom: How can you build trust by being appropriately transparent?

LaChelle: The opposite of transparent is wearing a mask. I've noticed that people are wearing masks often. When you're in a business meeting, you don't want to talk about how your business may be losing money. There are elephants in the room that people want to avoid talking about.

People can trust you when you're dealing with reality, and that's a situation of good and bad.

People can feel more at ease with you because your mask is down.

Even if you come in contact with someone who is really positive and you resonate with that person, you can still have, at the back of your mind, the sense that this is too good to be true. You think, "They resonate with me. Here's a nice person." But you still wait for the other shoe to drop. It appears that we're conditioned by society to be wary that somebody is hiding something. Things are just not what they appear to be. This has an impact on how we relate to other people.

I recommend that you avoid being so guarded. This disarms people because they are impressed that someone doesn't have a problem in admitting that they went through a tough situation. If the other person sees that it's not a hang up for you, they see how you have real confidence. Your skillset is more credible. They feel like they really see you as a person and that they know you a lot better than just having a surface conversation.

Tom: Based on your experiences, how are you able to help your clients?

LaChelle: Having gone through tough times now helps me to really *see* other people. Before, I couldn't really see people because I was caught up in my own issues. I would be caught up in half-listening. My mind was caught up in fears of not being a good mom. "Am I being a good wife? Am I doing this right?" All of these different questions.

So now I'm able to have clarity and focus. I'm being genuine and intentional when meeting people. I can focus on the conversation. I can focus one hundred percent on the other person.

And, I'm able to notice certain patterns and help my clients to avoid certain tough outcomes. A friend of mine, a psychologist, speaks of "the patterns that we do determine our behaviors."

You become aware of the pattern of not really knowing your own voice. It's evidenced in not being able to establish boundaries. You're not able to say *no* to certain things. This comes up because you want to please other people. You really don't have a clear sense of who you are. So, you're thinking that the easiest thing is to just please other people. If somebody calls you, you're jumping.

You're measuring things by outside appearances. Some people look at what a successful person does, and it looks effortless. It's important not to just go by the outside appearance and think you can just imitate that person's success.

When you work with a coach, you look inside and value what you bring to the table.

You focus on being who you are, and then you perform at your maximum potential.

LaChelle Adkins, also known as "America's SuperMom," has created a movement to empower women to overcome stress, depression and limiting beliefs.

LaChelle and her husband Jerome have 15 children (13 of which they had together) and 2 sons from other relationships. LaChelle has experience with juggling motherhood, military family life, career and life in the ministry, all of which led to a search for perfection which was unobtainable. This quest to acquire something not possible led to a downward spiral of depression which resulted in three hospitalizations.

After the last hospitalization in 2016, LaChelle decided to walk away from the victim mindset and embrace a victory mindset in order to teach others to successfully overcome these obstacles in their lives. She created a strategy she coined as "Fresh" start (https://bit.ly/2KxKmuJ) that allowed her to overcome stress, depression and limiting beliefs.

LaChelle serves as a life coach, guiding clients in how to implement this strategy to overcome similar obstacles in their lives. She believes her success is due to her ability to be transparent with her clients, which builds trust and helps them to be comfortable while removing masks and emotional walls.

She currently has programs for one on one coaching, group coaching, and she does public speaking. Her platform has extended beyond her business to include community outreach with such organizations as Haven House, Children's Hospital of Atlanta, Communities in Schools (https://bit.ly/2KAtjs2)

Henry County Schools and a National 30-day organizational campaign alongside Rachael Ray and organizing guru Peter Walsh.

LaChelle feels grateful for her challenges because they have allowed her to serve and add value in the lives of others. Her experiences have helped her to be focused, empathetic and comfortable being herself without seeking validation from others.

LaChelle can be followed at
https://www.lachelleadkins.com
and on LinkedIn and Facebook.

* * * * * *

Be Heard-20 Method #3

Run in Better Races

Years ago, I was feeling overwhelmed. I told my sweetheart, "I'm like a racehorse."

"Run in better races," she replied, encouraging me to be more selective.

Good point. This led to my idea: *I need to be in an area*

where a big payday is possible.

This proved to be true the first time I earned $1,000 in one hour. At the time I was earning $14 an hour as a marketing assistant.

My question was: *Is there something I can do that comes easy to me, but is hard for other people—and people will pay me to do it?*

Write down your own possible answers to this question, which I will repeat: Is there something I can do that comes easy to me, but is hard for other people—and people will pay me to do it?

I knew I could study, synthesize information, and convey it in an entertaining way.

Acclaimed television host Johnny Carson said, "People will pay more to be entertained than to be educated." So, I earned $1000 in one hour by speaking to a group on a topic which I had never presented before. (This was so many years ago.)

An interviewer commented, "It sounds like it takes chutzpah and courage to try new things and put yourself at risk."

Often, **one needs to act with courage.** My audiences like my phrase, *Courage is easier when I'm prepared.* The point is that I prepare every day for my next speech, interview or book that I write. In recent years, I often read up to 82 books in one year. I prepare by keeping up with my fields of interest.

How does one get into a better race?

It's about your skills in building relationships. And the essence of effective networking (for jobs and more) is building good relationships. Many opportunities that I have enjoyed have come from building business and personal relationships. Years ago, my first opportunity to be marketed by a speaker bureau at the $5,000 level came from years of building a relationship with the bureau's team members. This is how you get in a better race. You are friendly, trustworthy and helpful in all your dealings with people. Then people bring you opportunities.

Along the line of building relationships, Natalie Glebova reveals insights about coming across with confidence and authenticity.

Interview with Natalie Glebova

Tom: To come across as confident and trustworthy, what does a person need to do?

Natalie: On a more spiritual level, I would say that in order to be confident and trustworthy, *be authentic.* That's the number one important thing.

The common cliché is to "be yourself." But what does this really mean? Being yourself means being present with yourself and being present with this moment.

You're being in touch with your body and in touch with your emotions. Don't let the thoughts overtake you. Feel the true essence of who you are. By focusing on your breathing and feeling the life inside of your body, you can experience and feel what it is like to be overtaken and to surrender to the present moment.

I believe that this is the key to appearing authentic and to convey your truth to other people. So, whatever you say comes from a place *not* driven by your ego. It's not driven by some concepts in your mind. But it's from a true place within yourself. That's the number one thing I recommend.

Tom: To appear confident and trustworthy, what is best for someone to *avoid*?

Natalie: Pay attention to your body language. Don't fidget. Don't play with your hands.

Instead of appearing like you're nervous, be still and be calm. Place your hands firmly on the table or at your sides as you *avoid* doing something constantly with your hands.

This is important because when people see you fidgeting, they get this feeling that you are nervous—or maybe you're trying to hide something. You seem *not* confident and that you're not really being yourself.

Tom: I have a follow-up question. There are people I talk with—someone comes up to me after I give a speech, and I would tell them the truth that you shared, *be yourself.* And, they would say, "This self? This nervous self I have? This scared self. If I was just tuned into the scared part of myself, then I don't think I could convince anyone of anything." So how do you make a shift to the true self?

Natalie: It doesn't happen overnight. In very rare cases you might be able to make a shift like a giant quantum leap from one mindset to another. It usually comes from experience and a lot of inner work. It comes with time, I believe.

But you can't just say, "I'm going to give it time." You have to actually do something in order to change your mindset and change the way you behave. So, you can write a list of things that scare you and journal about them to understand your feelings.

It helps to meditate every single day and visualize yourself as how you want to conduct yourself—in a public setting—a speech or a small group at your work or social circle.

A lot of deep introspection is needed to understand one's

fear about how people are perceiving you or judging you. That's why I recommend journaling about your feelings to let them out. You can acknowledge that they're there, and then you meditate on that feeling. Every day meditate at least 10 to 15 minutes—more if you can. I recommend 30 minutes. Observe your thoughts and feelings about the situation. Just allow them to be—before you release them.

You pay attention to your feelings, and you actually acknowledge them without judging them. You feel them. What is this tightness in my chest or anxiety feeling in the pit of my stomach? Watch yourself become aware of that feeling, and it will dissolve. Whenever I'm anxious about something, I close my eyes and I go deep down into the feeling—and when I am conscious of it without any judgment and observe it—it quickly disappears on its own.

You have to meditate and do introspective work on yourself every day. Then put yourself out there into the situations that make you uncomfortable. Because the only way to grow is to put yourself out of your comfort zone to experience new things firsthand.

Tom: Knowing what you know now, what would you have done differently?

Natalie: I was shy when I was younger. At 13, I arrived as a Russian immigrant in Canada. I had the lowest self-esteem.

Knowing what I know now, if I could talk to my younger self, I would say,

"Always look for a different perspective. Any opinion you have of yourself or someone else, there is another angle you can look from."

So, your job is to find that other angle, even if you don't believe it at the moment.

If you have a limiting belief about yourself, it helps to ask, "Is this really true?" Often, the answer is, "No, this belief is *not* true." You'll learn to tell yourself, "There's another angle here. Or there's another angle over there."

Whether you think that you're not good enough or that you're shy or that you're not worthy—you can always disprove that limiting belief.

And the way to disprove a limiting belief is to replace it with an empowering new belief and then take action based on this new belief.

For example, my parents, as Russian immigrants, gave me some limiting beliefs about my being Russian and *not* being good enough.

But I decided to look at it from another perspective, and I realized that there are many Russians who are intelligent, cultured and sophisticated. I even started to believe that Russian girls are sexy, like the Bond girls in spy movies.

So, I chose to use these new empowering beliefs.

I realized that I wanted to let go of the limiting beliefs because they were *not* serving me.

So, what did I need to do? I needed to switch to the empowering beliefs that I learned from some positive people.

Even though in the beginning, I might have not believed the empowering beliefs, I resolved: *"I am going to do it, anyway."*

I learned to improve my inner dialogue. I spend a few minutes everyday instilling a new, empowering belief in myself. I choose what I focus on with my mind.

Find something in yourself that you really love and appreciate and focus more on *that*.

Remember, confidence and assertiveness come with experience and with time. The more you put yourself out there in situations where you feel uncomfortable—but you do it, anyway—the more your confidence builds.

Continue practicing your mindfulness, awareness, meditation and presence.

Natalie Glebova is an empowerment coach, author and former Miss Universe. She has been intensely focused on women empowerment and gender equality activism for the last decade. As a He4She advocate, a campaign by UN Women, she is very passionate about encouraging young people to build their self-confidence and reach their biggest goals. She is currently teaching a course "Empowered YOU" at Bangkok University to international students about effective goal-setting, mastering self-discipline, finding a purpose in life, and positive thinking.

Graduate of IT Management from Ryerson University in Toronto, Canada, she also has a certificate in Nutrition and Sport from Washington State University. Natalie has been actively involved in charity work ever since she moved to Thailand in 2006, and was a spokesperson for world-wide and local organizations including Habitat for Humanity and Operation Smile.

She has written two best-selling books: *Healthy Happy Beautiful* and *I AM WINNING—A Guide to Personal Empowerment.* Her public seminars and online empowerment training courses are centered around having the habits and the mindset that will make you a winner in life. https://natalieglebova.com

* * * * * *

Be Heard-20 Method #4

How to Be Liked

We often come across the classic idea that one needs the other person to know you, like you and trust you.

People will do a lot for a friend. In directing a feature film, I expanded the part of the little girl who portrayed the daughter of the main character because I liked her and her parents. They were a joy to work with. I had no hesitation in rewriting the script to expand her part.

On the other hand, I have worked with people who were disruptive. I arranged the schedules so that they were off my movie set quickly.

Being likeable is a big component in getting a job, a movie role, an investment into your project and other opportunities. (You can call this *The Liking Factor*.) How can you encourage someone new to like you?

Use the L.I.K.E.–M.E.–N.O.W. process:

L – Listen
I – Interview
K – Kindle similarity
E – Express gratitude
M – Monitor time
E – Engage the person's concerns
N – Note ideal clients
O – Open to humor
W – Watch and help

Listen – Listen first. Ask a gentle question such as, "So, how do you know our host, Matt?"

Interview – You can easily start a conversation and put

the person at ease with a gentle question. Pick a question that is easy and even pleasant to answer. At a conference, you can ask, "Oh, is there someone you're really looking forward to hearing?" At a social gathering, I might ask, "When you're taking it easy, do you like to read or see movies?" Asking "What are your hobbies?" can be helpful because people frequently enjoy their hobbies more than their current jobs. Or you can ask, "What are you looking forward to?"

Kindle similarity – A conversation warms up when people have a "I've experienced that, too!" moment. You often you hear this kind of comment: "Oh, you like skiing, too? What's your favorite resort?"

Express gratitude – You can say, "Thanks for your time," or "Thank you for your efforts on this one." In an e-mail, it often helps to begin with "Thank you for … "

Monitor time – Respect the person's time. Say things like, "This will be quick. I know you're busy."

Engage the person's concerns – Ask gentle questions to find out what is causing pain or inconvenience for the person. Then you can show how you hold similar concerns. This creates connection.

Note ideal clients – You can ask, "Who's your ideal client?" or "Are you looking for specific types of people? Perhaps, I can help send some folks your way."

Open to humor – Humor is something to be careful about. In fact, in one of my previous books, I covered 30 Secrets of Humor. I emphasize that it is helpful to observe what the person finds funny and flow with it if possible. One author states that the people he loves are the ones he laughs with.

Watch and help – You can ask, "How can I be supportive of what you're doing?" This is a better question than "How can I help you?" because many of us recoil when hearing a salesperson ask that question in a brick-and-mortar store.

Create more Trust and Connect Well

The process is to *Note Value and Gratitude.* Remind the person of the value and benefits she will enjoy now that she has agreed to your proposal. This helps the sale or negotiated agreement stay solid. Remember, each sale or negotiated agreement is ideally part of a good long-term business relationship.

The second point is to effectively thank the person for working with you. People appreciate a heartfelt "thank you." The crucial thing to remember is that each individual has a preferred way to receive appreciation and gratitude.

Along this line, while researching how people build healthy relationships, I discovered Dr. Gary Chapman's book, *The Five Love Languages.* In this book, Gary Chapman points out that each person has a personal "love language." If you speak the person's language, he or she will truly experience your gratitude. Here, I will focus on these love languages: Words of affirmation, Gifts, Quality time, and Acts of service. (The fifth language does *not* apply to our conversation here.)

Our goal is to appropriately and effectively express gratitude and create positive feelings.

You want to express your gratitude in a way the person can readily accept and feel. Here are examples related to the love languages:

Words of affirmation – "Joe, thanks for all your efforts. You were really effective in finding solutions to help our two teams work together. Thank you."

Gifts – A small, appropriate gift that relates to the person's hobby can be helpful. It's great when we honor people this way.

Quality time – When meeting with a new customer, turn off your cell phone. When someone acts as though taking a cell phone call is more important than talking to us, it hurts. Don't let this happen with your new customer.

Acts of service – Often, a customer will appreciate receiving a link to an article or YouTube video that relates to the hobby of her son or daughter. In this way, you can enrich your business relationship with the customer. The idea of service is that you extend an extra effort for the other person's well-being.

Remember, the idea is to effectively express gratitude and create good, friendly feelings.

An important part of creating a good interaction with another person is to learn to shift your own internal state. We'll now learn from Dr. Ginny Whitelaw's insights.

How You Can Release Stress and Build Trust in Relationships
An Interview with Dr. Ginny Whitelaw

Tom: How can we release ourselves from feeling overwhelmed?

Dr. Ginny: We get a sense of feeling overwhelmed when we're fighting with time. That's when we're trying to take on too much and cram it into time slots. We're racing through our day. We feel that things are heaping on top of us, and we go into a coping mode. It may sound ironic, but the solution is to drop into time. We slow down and breathe with it rather than fight with it. The sensation of how to do that is to start inside out, slow down your breathing, which is one of the fundamental frequencies informing your experience of calm vs overwhelm.

Life does not ask us to exhaust ourselves. Instead, we're exhausting ourselves by trying to do too much, with too much forced effort. It's better to relax into what is really called for right now—in this moment. We become more naturally sensitive to what is happening in this moment. This is what happens when we slow our breathing down—and drop into time and pay attention.

Tom: What new angle or advice would you offer for building trust in relationships?

Dr. Ginny: In building trust, and having communication that resonates, there's a deep sense of listening that is necessary. This is how we connect with another person and get on the same wavelength.

We have to sense them. We have to sense where they're coming from. Like ripples on the water, when we slow down our vibration it's easier to sense and reflect another person. We listen for and feel for where the other person is coming from. Once we match their energy then we might want to take it this way or that. We don't necessarily have to stay in their original energy pattern, but we do have to go there to join. We create a basic kind of resonance or harmony. The neuroscience of this is clear. Communication that is resonant occurs as your brain and my brain actually start to synchronize. This is the condition that builds trust—because you feel heard and I feel heard.

We start to get a sense of "I know what to expect from you." We start to make little maps of each other inside our own bodies. When we get what we expect, there's a sensation of "Yeah, I get this person." That builds trust.

On the other hand, if we are each stuck in our own positions or off in our own worlds and just bounce off of each other, that's when conflict arises and communication breaks down. Then, trust does not establish. We need to remember to have a deep sense of listening.

Tom: How can we make ourselves better heard?

Dr. Ginny: **Become better listeners,** because when we listen—and I'm going to the physics of this—we vibrate with someone. When we vibrate with someone, that means that we are making an internal map of them. We're getting a sense of them. We're taking them inside ourselves. This mostly passes beneath conscious awareness, but it's happening anyway.

When we match what we say to what we're hearing and we match frequencies, then we can be heard. We don't bounce off and deflect, with the other person coming back saying, "Huh? What?" And, if we do get that reaction, we notice it because we are in tune. We can pause and say, "Wait, I think I just said something that thudded with you. Let's go back …" So, we can start to play in that dialogue. When people feel listened to and heard, they get smarter, and they get more generous. They get more open. They relax more. They get connected.

In this time of technology speeding us up, it's necessary for us to slow down, which means slow down our breathing, pace ourselves, fall into time, not fight with it. With the right inner condition, we avoid being distracted by the noise, texts, emails and more.

Dr. Ginny Whitelaw is the founder and CEO of the Institute for Zen Leadership, a Zen Master in Rinzai Zen, as well as President of Focus Leadership. A biophysicist by training, she combines a deep scientific background with senior leadership experience at NASA, and 25 years coaching and developing global leaders. She is a recognized expert in leadership development and mind-body, and has written several books, including The Zen Leader and Move to Greatness. She also co-developed the FEBI®, which measures 4 patterns in the nervous system linking mind, body and behaviors, and trains practitioners worldwide in applying FEBI in their work.

Dr. Whitelaw spent 10 years at NASA, where she became the Deputy Manager for integrating the International Space Station, for which she received NASA's Exceptional Service Medal. She holds a Ph.D. in Biophysics, as well as a B.S. in Physics, a B.A. in Philosophy, and a 5th degree black belt in Aikido. http://www.zenleader.global

Principle: Develop positive business relationships. Help the person feel good by showing the value gained through your presence and by expressing your gratitude.

Power Questions: How can you gently remind the person of the value he or she has gained? How can you express your gratitude?

* * * * * *

Be Heard-20 Method #5

Continually prepare for the home run

We never know when a great, new opportunity will arrive. That detail inspires us to *prepare daily for the big opportunity* that can create a *home run* in terms of our personal success.

For example, nearly every day of the year, I am

rehearsing, writing and improving my material for speeches and books. I'm learning from mentors daily.

Now, billionaire Andres Pira, a master of seizing opportunities, shares his insights …

Interview with Andres Pira

Tom: What does it take to rise to high levels of achievement?

Andres Pira: I like setting 101 goals. Most people have to understand that you have to put small goals into any goal setting because when you only have bigger goals, they become very hard to obtain. Blend small goals with big goals. Because as soon as you complete small goals, it feels like you're moving forward, and then you can go to the bigger goal. You have the sense of moving forward every time. It gives you more confidence to achieve the bigger goals.

In my book, *Homeless to Billionaire*, I write about full-color goal setting. Many people set unspecific goals like gain a million dollars. It's very hard to get something if it is not clear in your mind. If you want a new car, what color is it? How does it look inside? How does it smell? How often will you drive it? How will it feel? So, you need to be specific with any goal setting. And, that's how it will come much quicker to you.

Tom: What is an essential practice for creating success?

Andres: I believe that if you want success make other people successful. If it's money you want, help other people make money. If you want love, make sure to love yourself. Whatever you give comes back to you tenfold.

Tom: What's next for you?

Andres: I consider myself a global citizen. Although I've built my empire in Southeast Asia, I don't see any possibilities within this world that are out of reach. The mind-set is the most important gift I can contribute positively to both local and global society. A progressive shifting mind-set from one person can make a wave. This is the moment. Now is the time I would like to be a contributor to the change-making movements.

Andres Pira is the author, with Dr. Joe Vitale, of the book, *Homeless to Billionaire: The 18 Principles of Wealth Attraction And Creating Unlimited Opportunity.* Becoming a millionaire at thirty was only the beginning for Swedish billionaire, entrepreneur, speaker and author Andres Pira. At the age 35, Pira went on to gain a net worth of that of a billionaire! Based in Phuket, Thailand, his group of companies under Blue Horizon Developments is currently a luxury resort empire of 19 companies with 249 employees and growing. A serial businessman, his portfolio spans real estate, gyms, a law office, gas station, coffee shops, and live events company. Blue Horizon Developments has received over fifteen awards from internationally-acclaimed property awards groups such as International Property Awards, Thailand Property, and Dot Property Group. A philanthropist at heart, Pira believes one's true wealth is the good one does in this world. In his spare time, Pira enjoys mountain climbing, skydiving, bungee jumping, skiing, bodybuilding, and football. https://andrespira.com

A vital part of preparation is identifying what you truly want. Here are Marc Allen's (author, president and publisher of New World Library) comments on his discoveries about *creating a life you truly love:*

Move Beyond Abundance to a Life of True Fulfillment by Marc Allen

The first step to discovering the secret of manifestation is to write your ideal scene on paper, your dream life five years in the future. Begin with the end in mind and keep it in mind. The day I turned thirty, I sat down and took a sheet of paper and wrote Ideal Scene at the top. I imagined everything had gone as well as I could possibly imagine and somehow, over the next five years, I was able to create the ideal life for me. What would it look like? What would I do and have, and who would I be?

I was surprised, even shocked in a strange way, at what came spilling out on paper. I imagined I had a publishing company, successfully publishing books and music, including my own books and music. Before I sat down and wrote out my ideal scene, I had absolutely no interest in business. I had never taken a business course. I had never written a book or recorded my music. The words that spilled out when I wrote my ideal scene surprised me as much as they were to surprise just about everyone else I knew.

I imagined I wrote successful books and recorded beautiful music as well. I imagined I had a lovely white house on a hill in northern California, one of my favorite places on earth. I imagined I had a wonderfully loving relationship. I dared to imagine my ideal, so I imagined I had plenty of time for it all: creativity, a successful business, friends and family, and plenty of time alone for myself as well … That was my ideal: success with ease, and success without compromising the other things that were important to me in life …

The second step to discovering the secret of manifestation is to write your goals as affirmations, beginning with "In an easy and relaxed manner, in a healthy and positive way … " Years later, looking back, I realized how powerful those words were—so powerful, in fact, that by repeating them daily, I overcame many of my doubts and fears …

The next step to discovering the secret of manifestation is to write a one-page plan for every major goal …

The final step to discovering the secret of manifestation is to take action …

We know the secret, deep in our hearts. We've always known the secret. To love one another and all of creation, is the greatest secret of all. Love overcomes fear and transforms our lives and our world.

Marc Allen is a renowned author and president and publisher of New World Library, which he co-founded with Shakti Gawain in 1977. Guiding the company from a small start-up with no capital to its current position as one of the leading independent publishers in the country, Marc has shepherded some of the most influential non-fiction books of the past 30 years, including *The Power of Now* by Eckhart Tolle, *The Seven Spiritual Laws of Success* by Deepak Chopra, and *Creative Visualization* by Shakti Gawain.

Marc is the author several life-changing books, including *Visionary Business, A Visionary Life, The Millionaire Course, The Greatest Secret of All*, the newly revised *Tantra for the West*, and his most recent publication *The Magical Path*.

As a gifted speaker and seminar leader, Marc works with people around the globe to craft lives of lasting abundance and prosperity. www.MarcAllen.com

Several people report that implementing Marc's suggestions allows one's possibilities to expand.

Principle: Devote time and effort daily to preparing for upcoming opportunities.

Power Question: What might be a terrific opportunity that you need to prepare for now—before such an opportunity is offered?

* ** * * *

Be Heard-20 Method #6

How you can use the Internet for networking

Bestselling author Guy Kawasaki uses his blog to solidify relationships with his current customer base and with new people who come into his Web site via Google.com and other search engines. When I contacted Guy about a previous edition of *Be Heard and Be Trusted*, I knew what a fast-moving person he is. He invited me to pick something that would fit from his blog. So, here is an excerpt from …

Guy's Blog … https://guykawasaki.com/blog/
October 25, 2007
A Night in the Life of Guy Kawasaki Plus Cool Stuff Friday
by Guy Kawasaki
It's 10:30 pm, and I'm sitting on a baggage cart on the tarmac of the Monterey, California airport. My U. S. Airways flight was set to depart and then an engine warning light went on—this was two hours ago. The reason we're all on

the tarmac is that a fire alarm went off, so we had to evacuate the terminal.

Still, this is better than the last time I flew on U.S. Airways. That time one of the plane's engines died, and we made an "unscheduled stop" in Kansas City and then had to wait four hours for another plane to fly in. What's all of the got to do with this entry? Nothing except that I've had two hours to compile a short list of cool stuff.

It's been one of those days. This afternoon I spoke for my buddies at Cisco [Systems]. Just before the speech, I discovered that the recently dry-cleaned pants that I packed were my son's, not mine, so I had to give the speech wearing jeans. One high point: Reggie Jackson was on the flight too, but he left after two hours of waiting. He was giving out autographs—though he didn't ask me for mine. :-) If I get to Las Vegas anytime soon, I'm speaking for the Entrepreneurs' Organization.

[At this point, Guy shared a number of links. It has been some time since then, so I'll forego reprinting the links here. The relevance of certain links diminishes.]

Here is a more recent excerpt from Guy's blog:

The Art of Branding

In the real world, you don't have infinite resources; you don't have a perfect product; and you don't sell to a growing market without competition. You're also not omnipotent, so you cannot control what people think of your brand. Under these assumptions, most companies need all the help they can get.

This is my advice to help you.

- **Seize the high ground.** Establish your brand on positive conditions like "making meaning," "doing good," "changing the world," and "making people happy" —not destroying your competition. When is the last time you bought a product to hurt a company's competition? (Other than maybe Macintosh users.) If you want to beat your competition, establish an uplifting brand but don't try to establish a brand based on a silly desire to destroy your competition.

- **Create one message.** It's hard enough to create and communicate one branding message; however, many companies try to establish several because they want the "entire" market and are afraid of being niched. "Our computer is for Fortune 500 companies. And, oh yes, it's also for consumers to use at home." Face it, Volvo can't equal safety (not rolling over) and sexiness, and Toyota can't equal economical and lexuriousness {sic}. So, pick one message, stick with it for at least a year if it appears promising, and then try another. But you can't try several at once or switch every few months.

- **Speak English.** Not necessarily "English," but speak in non-jargonese. If your positioning statement uses any acronyms, the odds are that (a) most people won't understand your branding, and (b) your branding won't last long. For example, "best MP3decoder" presumes that people understand what "MP3" and "decoder" mean much less the term "MP3" itself. Not to be an ageist, but a good test is to ask your parents if they understand what your positioning means—assuming your parents aren't computer science professors.

- **Take the opposite test.** How many times have you read a product description like this? "Our software is scalable, secure, easy-to-use, and fast?"

Companies use these adjectives as if no other company claims its product is scalable, secure, easy-to-use, and fast. Unless your competition uses the antonyms of the adjectives that you use, your description is useless. I've never seen a company say that its product was limited, vulnerable, hard-to-use, and slow.

- **Cascade the message.** Let's say that you craft the perfect branding message. As the Jewish say, "Mazel tov." Now cascade your message up and down your organization. The marketing departments of many companies assume that once they've put out the press release or run the ad, the entire world understands the message. It's unlikely that even the company does. Start with your board of directors and work down to Trixie and Biff at the front desk and make sure every employee understands the branding.

- **Examine the bounce back.** You know what messages you send, but you really don't know what messages people receive. Here's a concept: you should ask them to bounce back the message that you sent so that you can learn how your message is truly interpreted. In the end, it's not so much what you say as much as what people hear.

- **Focus on social media, not advertising.** Many companies waste away millions of dollars trying to establish brands with advertising. Too much money is worse than too little because when you have a lot of money, you spend a lot of money on stupid things like Super Bowl commercials. Brands are built on what people are saying about you on social media, not what you're saying about yourself. People say good things about you when (a) you have a great product and (b) you get people to spread the word about it.

- **Strive for humanness.** Great brands achieve a high level of humanness.{click to tweet} They speak to you as an individual, not as part of a market. It's "my iPod," "my Macintosh," "my Harley Davidson" and "my bottle of Coke." By contrast, no one thinks, "My Microsoft Office," so I wouldn't label Microsoft as a great brand although kids think of "My xBox." Unfortunately for Microsoft, "xBox" and "Microsoft" are not closely linked to each other.

Now step back and ask yourself the $64,000 question: "If we don't spend a dime on marketing, will people be aware of our brand and understand what it stands for?" Because the real world of marketing is this: you don't have a big marketing budget, so you have to depend on people "creating" your brand for you.

Guy Kawasaki is the chief evangelist of Canva, (an online design service) and an executive fellow of the Haas School of Business at the University of California, Berkeley. Previously, he was the chief evangelist of Apple and special adviser to the CEO of the Motorola business unit of Google. His many acclaimed books include *The Art of Social Media* and *Enchantment.* He lives in Silicon Valley with his family and on social media where he has ten million followers.

Kawasaki has a BA from Stanford University and an MBA from UCLA as well as an honorary doctorate from Babson College. www.GuyKawasaki.com

More methods for working with Social Media

If you want to build a ship, don't herd people together to collect wood and don't assign them tasks and work, but rather teach them to long for the endless immensity of the sea.
– Antoine De Saint Exupery

Antoine's comment inspires us to touch people's hearts and create a feeling of longing in them.

Communicating—especially via social media—involves capturing the viewer's attention.

An old journalistic comment is, "If it bleeds, it leads." We notice that news broadcasts often begin with intense stories about hurricanes and other calamities.

If you can show people how to protect themselves from loss, you can seize their attention.

Perfection is achieved, not when there is nothing more to add, but when there is nothing left to take away.
– Antoine De Saint Exupery

Simplicity counts. We live in a sound bite culture. You need to get your message down to a simple, clear, hard-hitting point. "Your brand is the shortest distance to trust," I advised the audience of my sixth annual presentation to the National Association of Broadcasters Conference, in Las Vegas.

Being positive with a simple message works in certain situations. About 20 years later, I still remember one link on Oprah.com The link stated simply *Get Better Sleep*. I clicked on this link.

* ** * * *

Be Heard-20 Method #7

Great Communicators Give Compelling Speeches

What would you do if you were terrified of speaking before a group? Would you become a professional speaker? That's what I did.

How did I make the transition? When I was in grammar school, I was pushed to play the piano for thirty-one elderly people living in a senior-care facility. I sat down and my leg began to shake so fast—like a hummingbird's wings. I felt sure they could see my terror. My foot shook so hard that I was afraid it would fall off the pedal with an embarrassing *thud.* I was focused on the thoughts, "How am I doing? They've heard these songs before. My playing is not that good. They'll wince at all the wrong notes."

My fear of public performance has been part of my path to be a public speaker who entertains thousands of people from Silicon Valley, California to New York to Thailand and New Zealand—and more.

I had to learn techniques to handle my fears. When I speak now, my focus is, *"How may I serve?"* I let go of the thought, "How am I doing?"

To make things better, it is crucial that you take action. To give good speeches, here's my action: *I rehearse.* Anytime I feel uneasy about an upcoming speech, I rehearse for a few moments.

Jay Conrad Levinson shares similar insights about taking action:

Instantly
by Jay Conrad Levinson

I make tough situations better by eliminating them ASAP each time. One of life's greatest satisfactions for me seems to be throwing things away. Although you'd never know it to look around my home, I seem to be dedicated to removing stuff from my files, computer desktop, real desktop, in-basket, and to-do list. At the end of every workday, which means Monday through Wednesday to me, I delight in crossing the final task off the list in my datebook.

At the end of every year, I cross the line into true ecstasy when I fill several full-sized garbage cans with paper no longer needed. I feel pretty much the same when I relieve my hard drive of data nobody on earth will ever need again. I've learned that by dealing with work assignments only one time, I am able to gain a lot more precious free time for myself. Instead of putting the work aside for a later date, I deal with it at the moment it comes in, so that I won't have to be involved with it ever again. People say that I'm a good e-mail correspondent. I answer that it's mainly because I don't like having e-mail to answer. That's why I'm getting back to you instantly.

Jay Conrad Levinson was the author of the bestselling marketing series in history, *Guerrilla Marketing*, plus 56 other business books. His books have sold over 21 million copies worldwide. And his guerrilla concepts have influenced marketing so much that his books appear in 43 languages and are required reading in MBA programs worldwide.

If you are called on to give a speech, it helps to follow Jay's example and take action instantly—that is, rehearse.

If you are confronted with the situation of needing to give a speech within one week, or even within five minutes, you can use the following S.P.E.E.C.H. process:

S – Summarize

P – Prepare your first sentence and last sentence

E – Express an anecdote

E – Enter with a benefit

C – Conclude with "Thank you"

H – Honor three memorable points

1. Summarize

What is the most important point, which you want your audience to remember for weeks after your speech?

Imagine how great you would feel if someone came up to you one year later and said, "I heard your speech, and I will always remember that you said ..." This is what happened for speaker/author Hyrum Smith, CEO and cofounder of Franklin Quest Company (prior to a later merger). Hyrum gave a speech, and one year later he received this letter:

Hyrum, I went to your seminar a year ago in Princeton. It never occurred to me that what I do on a daily basis ought to be based on my governing values ... the things that really matter most to me ... I decided to dedicate my life to making a good life for my son [here he describes several activities shared with his son] ... Hyrum, last week my son, eight years old, was killed in an automobile accident. I have experienced some real pain at the loss of my son. But I have to tell you that I have experienced no guilt ... Hyrum, thank you.

Inspired by Hyrum's speech, this father had taken action to make a good life for his son. To make a powerful impact such as this, we must know our **most important point.** That point will be a highlight of the summary at the end of the speech.

Your summary creates the powerful ending you desire. I emphasize to my clients that a good speech ends with the speaker in control. Avoid ending with a question-and-answer period. A Q&A session has a puttering-out effect.

Instead, prepare for your ending by writing down three memorable points. At the end of your speech, say something like: "And now I will summarize. First, remember to … Second, we do better when we … And finally, you make a great impact by … Thank you."

Speak properly, and in as few words as you can, but always plainly; for the end of speech is not ostentation, but to be understood. – William Penn

A proverb is much matter distilled into few words.
– Buckminster Fuller

Do not say a little in many words, but a great deal in a few.
– Pythagoras

Principle: End with strength. Summarize your points.
Power Question: What are your three main points? (Write down a strong way to repeat those points in a summary.)

2. *Prepare Your First Sentence and Your Last Sentence*
Did you ever attend a speech that the speaker simply read? Have you endured watching a speaker stare at the back wall as he spoke, as if his speech was plastered on that wall?

I advise my graduate students to avoid memorizing each word of a speech. Instead, we want the presentation to have a rapport-creating naturalness. It helps to start strongly with a memorized first sentence and end powerfully with a memorized last sentence.

For your first sentence, you can begin with:

- A question
- A powerful fact
- A detail that moves emotions

Be sincere; be brief; be seated. – President Franklin D. Roosevelt

Principle: People remember the beginning and end of your speech. Start and finish with strength.

Power Questions: What is a strong first sentence for your speech? Note three possibilities. What is a memorable last sentence for your speech? Note three possibilities.

3. Express an Anecdote

How do you get past a person's natural resistance? Tell a story. Here we will designate an anecdote as a "story with a point." In fact, a powerful way to state clearly the value of a story is to end it with "And so, my point is …" or to conclude with "What I learned that day was …"

What we observe is not nature itself, but nature exposed to our method of questioning. – Werner Heisenberg (physicist)

Related to Heisenberg's comment, we see that our story is like a "method of questioning." When questioning something, we are actually forming our own version of a story. Choose your questions well to set the direction of your story. The anecdote touches the hearts of your audience in ways that logic and rational arguments cannot.

We're not seeing what's real; we just see our story.
– Tom Marcoux

A good, heartfelt story helps you give the audience a new view of reality. The story provides an experience in which the audience can invest their emotions. Carefully select three anecdotes and try them with friends and family. Find out which anecdote reaches people's hearts.

Principle: Express an anecdote to seize attention and change lives.

Power Question: How can you make your point with an anecdote that inspires minds and moves emotions?

4. Enter with a Benefit

Picture an audience of jobseekers watching a speaker taking the stage. Her first words are: "Imagine you could make $1,000 *a minute* in a job interview. That's what we're going to cover today."

Does she have their attention? Yes.

When you start a speech, the listener subconsciously asks the **3 W's:**

1. Who are you?
2. Why should I listen to you?
3. What's in it for me?

Answer these questions. You seize the listeners' attention and walk the path to be heard and be trusted.

Researchers report that people will put out more effort to avoid a loss than to gain joy. When addressing a class of MBA students, I illustrated this point by placing a $10 bill on my left knee and a $20 bill on my right knee. I mimed having the $10 snatched away. I then asked, "What will people put more effort into, avoiding the loss of $10 or gaining $20?" The students replied, "Not losing the $10." They were correct. Students told me that this illustration makes a visceral impact, driving home the point that **we're all interested in** *avoiding loss.*

Hard-charging people are concerned about *the loss of time.* They fear things that "waste their time."

Focus on being productive rather than being busy—your life depends on it. – Timothy Ferris

Show people how they will save time, gain leverage, and get more done, and you have their attention. When you focus your speech on *the vital few,* your audience will bless you. By *the vital few,* I mean the three major points that provide compelling benefits for your audience. I emphasize three benefits because that gives you three chances that any given audience member will find one of the benefits to be compelling.

* * * * * *

Be Heard-20 Method #8

Get Clear on the Value You Bring to the Table

A vital part of delivering a pitch is "the ask"—that's when you ask for what you want. I have worked with clients who were seeking $2 million to $6 million in a round of funding.

How can one be forthright and firm as he or she asks for something on the edge of their belief? **You need to know, deep in your gut, the value you are bringing to the table.**

The process involves asking yourself challenging

questions and making sure your answers move your own heart.

Even before raising funds, several people have trouble charging what is appropriate for their services.

Along this line, here's guidance from Jeanna Gabellini.

Why Clients Aren't Paying You What You're Worth
by Jeanna Gabellini

Darn near everyone gripes about money. I do it, too. We each have triggers about making, spending and saving money. But the one I hear the most about is not getting paid enough. Either you have an abundance of clients, but they don't pay you for the real value you give, or you don't have enough clients and you're scared to charge what you deserve.

You might not even know what you deserve because you've been brainwashed to take what you can get even if you only end up making twenty bucks an hour in the end. Maybe a few people gave you feedback that they can't afford your services and products and now you're convinced that nobody will buy at your current prices.

There are more than a few reasons why your ideal customers don't pay you what you're worth and it's not because they can't afford you! Think about it. If they're your ideal customers, then they see the value in what problem you solve and joyfully say *"yes"* to whatever price you set.

If you're not charging enough you may need to:

1. Figure out the real cost of doing business. Include all overhead and time spent for every little aspect of delivering

each product and service.

2. Nail down exactly what you need to take home each week.

3. Be more objective about the value your products and services give.

4. Lay out, on paper, the features and benefits of each product and service.

5. Charge from knowing what you want to grow into, not who you've been.

6. Consider yourself more of an expert in your field, even if you're a newbie. You bring something special to the table, no matter what stage of business growth you're in. When I was in coaches' training, I was serving up breakthroughs for my "practice" clients long before I got my first paying client.

If your prices seem congruent with the value your products and services deliver, and not enough people are buying, you may need to:

1. Nail down your *ideal* customer and stop marketing and saying "yes" to those who don't fit that description.

2. Look at your beliefs about success, struggle, wealth and making a profit from what you love doing most.

3. Check in about what you offer. Do you love what you offer and the way you serve it up? How does your business support your desired lifestyle?

4. Clearly lay out the benefits and features of what you offer on all marketing materials. If you don't have bullet points on sales pages or brochures you probably aren't spelling it out clearly.

5. You're trying too hard to get clients. Pushing, needing, and worrying about getting money in the door comes from a place of lack and won't yield an abundance of anything (except heartache).

6. Tap into your Inner Business Expert and ask, "How can I align with more ideal customers? What should I shift? Is there an action that would serve me in this desire?"

There are more than enough people out there to pay you what you are worth. Before you go killing yourself to try a bunch of new strategies to figure out how to attract them, sit with the suggestions above and feel into which ones may be perfect for you to put into action. One baby step at a time will be sufficient.

When it comes to client attraction it always starts with your beliefs. More than likely, you need to expect more. Make bigger financial goals and play to win. Play with confidence. Abundant expectancy without expectation.

Jeanna Gabellini is a Master Business Coach who assists conscious entrepreneurs to double (and even triple) their profits by leveraging attraction principles, proven strategies and fun. Grab her FREE audio on dialing in your biz at http://masterpeacecoaching.com/freecd

I included the above article because it notes how **we need to get insight into our** *inner game.*

To be at your best when fundraising or getting a new client, make sure that you have real clarity about the value you bring to the table.

Make sure you meet the investor as their peer. By this I mean, you are bringing great value to the conversation. You have *the prize—your startup and their opportunity to invest in it.* Beware that people feel contempt for "supplicants." Make sure your inner game is strong and you feel in your gut that you're bringing real value.

BONUS MATERIAL #1

Give a Great Speech with 2 Minutes of Preparation Time

Often, to get the attention of investors, you might be at a conference, and you have the chance to speak up in front of the room. The question is: "How am I going to say something with great content and also express my confidence?"

We'll use the W.I.N.S. process:

W – work out the first sentence and last sentence
I – intensify story
N – nurture a catchphrase
S – set a Solid, Fast Ending

1. Work out the first sentence and last sentence

People remember how you start and end your speech.

Choose your first sentence. Write it down so you can start strong. When you begin your speech with no hesitation, the audience has the subconscious feeling, "I'm in the hands of a pro."

When you work on both your first sentence and final sentence you can create **bookends.** It can sound like:

First sentence: "At 10:45 pm, as Sarah arrived home, she heard an unexpected and bad sound from the kitchen."

Final sentence: "Now, with XY Security System, at 10:45

pm, Sarah feels safe in her own home."

Using bookends and reminding us of what you started with can give your speech an extra, professional polish.

2. Intensify story

By *intensify story* I mean make sure your story has a clear point and that the audience knows the purpose for your story immediately. You can *intensify story* by saying, "This reminds me of a time when I learned..." Using this structure helps you get straight to the point and to announce that point before you deliver the story.

At the end of delivering the story, you can say, "That was an example of how I learned to..." In this way you have once again emphasized your point.

3. Nurture a catchphrase

Using a catchphrase can help you make what you say memorable. I have catchphrases including:
- To stand out, find out what you stand for.
- Keep score and achieve more.
- What you dread gets you ahead.
- Motion brings clarity.

Use your catchphrase well—that is, repeat it at least three times. You can close your speech by having the audience finish the catchphrase with you.

For example, for one of my speeches, in my final summary, I say: "So, remember ... Motion—"

"Brings clarity," the audience members say aloud.

"Excellent. You got it," I reply.

4. Set a Solid, Fast Ending

Sometimes, a big disappointment will give you the final

piece of a puzzle. For example, years ago, I felt disappointment crash on my head, while I was giving a speech during a competition. At first, things were going well. I was in the zone providing great, impromptu content. I even created five spontaneous humor bits that inspired the audience to laugh big time.

This completely through off my timing. My speech went on too long, and the speech was disqualified. Oww! It hurt.

After my speech, people came up and said, "Tom, you should have won."

I know I could have won with that speech, if I had only practiced saying, "That's what I want to share. Thank you."

You see that phrase is a *Solid, Fast Ending.*

I didn't have that ready. I had rehearsed other patterns that made my speech excellent.

However, I had failed to practice a Solid, Fast Ending.

Make sure you *rehearse patterns* of a Solid, Fast Ending.

The truth is your speech can be shut down at any time. You want to *avoid* appearing thrown off balance.

Here are examples of a Solid, Fast Ending:
- "Those are my thoughts on this. Thank you."
- "That's the last thing I'll share on this. Thank you."
- "With that—I say: Thank you."

Power Principle:
Use a quick outline based on the W.I.N.S. process.

Power Questions:
When will you apply this W.I.N.S. process?
W – work out the first sentence and last sentence
I – intensify story
N – nurture a catchphrase
S – set a Solid, Fast Ending

BONUS MATERIAL #2

Your Secret Charisma: Hidden Methods for Influence and Trust

As I delivered my speech, *Your Secret Charisma: Hidden Methods for Influence and Trust,* in New Zealand, I emphasized that **trust is the springboard for getting the support we need**. When you want investors to fund your project, you need access to what I call *Your Secret Charisma.*

We use the A.I.M.S. process:

A – agree and wonder
I – intensify how they convince themselves
M – magnify a story
S – set their permission

1. Agree and wonder

When I talk about *Warm Trust Charisma*, I emphasize that we create connection by reducing tension and helping the person feel that we're paying attention. We demonstrate that we care. How? You find something that you can sincerely point to and say, "I agree." It could be a simple expression of "I agree that is a vital area to focus on so we can come up with a solution."

Secondly, we can overcome an important problem. Often, when we're listening, we naturally judge what the person is saying. If you catch yourself judging something, you can imagine that the person feels judged at least on the subconscious level. The person may feel that something is off.

You can ask, "I wonder what is most important to you about _____?"

This demonstrates that the person's concerns are important to you.

Thirdly, you can use an alternative: "I'm curious. What is most important to you about _____?"

2. Intensify how they convince themselves

People do things for their own reasons and not for our reasons or logic that we press upon them. So, the method is to get the person to voice *their* reasons.

Certain researchers/authors came up with a process, which I'll demonstrate here:

Janet: "I think I should exercise more."

Marina: "How ready are you to exercise more—on a scale of 1 to 10? 10 is the highest. That is, you're most ready."

Janet: "6."

Marina: "Why isn't it a 2?"

Janet: "What?"

Marina: "Why isn't your level of being ready not as low as 2?"

Janet: "I…well, I want to protect myself from getting diabetes. My mother has it."

At this point, Janet *expresses her own reason* for exercising more.

In this way, Janet **starts to convince herself.**

3. Magnify a story

Telling a story is a powerful way to get a person to *experience* the value of your idea or proposal. However, many times, a listener is halfway into the story, and they're wondering: *"What is the point of this?"*

The solution is to begin with something like: "About a year ago, I learned that the best way to connect with an audience is _____." Then you tell the story.

You close with "And that's when I learned that the best way to connect with an audience is _____."

You mentioned the point before *and* after you expressed your story.

4. Set their permission

Some of us are afraid to sell something or make a strong pitch. Here is a solution ... Practice this phrase:

"Forgive me. I was just excited about the _____. How about we start over?"

I've learned this method from my own coaches. They ask for my permission to cover some material.

They may ask:

- "Tom, how about we go back to your experience when you were 22?"
- "Tom, you're okay if we go over that part when you said that _____ was bothering you?"

This process of gaining the person's permission grants you leeway to explore what will move the process along.

A Great Secret of Conversation

Be sure to help the other person feel comfortable and give the person space to express their *self* in conversation. I've shared this principle with MBA students and my clients:

When you're listening, you're winning.

The power of *Soft-hearted Persuasion* vs. *Hard-headed Convincing*

Hard-headed Convincing takes place when someone is when one tries to push their own reasons and logic on to another. They're trying to get the other person agree. However, the other person has a natural response of resisting.

On the other hand, *Soft-hearted Persuasion* is a process in which you ask questions to help the other person voice their own personal priorities and values.

Questions for Soft-hearted Persuasion:
- What matters to you about ___?
- What's most important to you about ____?

Here is a process* to help someone voice their real and personal reasons to take action:

You ask: "On a scale of 1-10, 10 being the highest, how ready are you to invest in this startup business?"
Investor: "Four."
You: "Why isn't it a two?"
Investor: "What?"
You: "Why are you at the level of two instead of zero?"
Investor: "Well, you do have some good traction with your first 10 paying clients. And …"

You notice that the above dialogue is unusual, and it helps the investor voice something positive about your offer.

* Some research about the value of this process is conveyed in the book *Instant Influence: How to Get Anyone to Do Anything—Fast* by Michael Pantalo

BONUS MATERIAL #3

Power Time Management for Gaining Funding

In my *Power Time Management: More Time, Less Stress and Zero Procrastination* workshop (with an audience at the Corporate Innovation Summit in Bangkok, Thailand), I emphasized that we would approach time management *in a different way.* Much of time management material emphasizes goals and lists.

On the hand, during that workshop I emphasized: "Leverage built on Relationships and Trust."

Use Questions to Help You Focus

As I work with clients who lead startup businesses in need of funding, I mentioned that Power Time Management includes gaining leverage by using vital questions:

1. *What are your current priorities?*
2. *What challenges/problems arose in the recent few days that you want solutions for?*
3. *What areas do you need big intuitive solutions for?*
4. *What concerns to do you have about the fundraising process in any facet?*
5. *What big meetings or pitch opportunities do you need rehearsals for?*

Power Time Management is about three things:
  • *More Time* – You get *more time* because you

eliminate unnecessary conflict. This is the process when you get the time back that would otherwise lose.

- *Less Stress* – Less stress comes from your having a Personal Energy Buffer.
- *Zero Procrastination* – Zero procrastination comes from intensifying systems and rehearsal. When I say, *intensify systems*, I mean you design a process so that you consistently get the most vital things done. And, that includes crucial rehearsal.

We realize one powerful action for becoming more confident is to rehearse. Rehearse before difficult conversations. Then you can avoid unnecessary escalation of conflict or misunderstanding.

Use Language to Save Time

I'm still impressed with how my associate art director commented on a book cover idea I had some time ago.

She said, "That's great art. It won't sell any books."

I understood her meaning immediately, and we moved away from my original book cover idea.

It's an example of great communication. My associate art director comment used what I call CCT—*Clarity, Compassion and Trust*.

When you can communicate in a similar CCT-way, you can save a lot of time.

I refer to this process as Power Time Management (and I also call it Confident Time Mastery).

We'll use the R.I.S.E. process:

R – rehearse and listen
I – intensify systems

S – say No with grace

E – energize *Good, Excellent and Amazing*

1. Rehearse and Listen

The way to have more leverage is to have better relationships. We do this by rehearsing before we have tough conversations.

What do we rehearse?

We can rehearse ways to defuse a situation and increase listening.

You can say something like:

- It sounds like you feel strongly about this. I'm interested in learning how you got to this perspective. Would you tell me more?
- Is there anything else you want me to know about this?

We listen because it is a fast way to enhance trust in a relationship—personal or business. (In other sections of this book, I teach methods to overcome Listening Blockers.)

Another form of "listening" is to listen to yourself.

I've learned that distilling your own wisdom and understanding is helpful to you can become more productive.

I've distilled much of what I've learned into catchprhases:

- Keep score and achieve more
- What you dread gets you ahead
- Being prepared for the worst often gets you the best
- Systems not willpower
- Think it through; rehearse it through

Perhaps, you said to yourself: "Okay. Makes sense."

Some people view comments like these as: "Too simple. I don't like formulas."

I suggest that you read this section through and pick up some method and implement it *(or at least rehearse it)* within five minutes of reading this section. That's how you gain the *most value.* (I use this phrase: "Squeeze the orange and get juice from it.)

2. Intensify Systems
(Design for Consistency and Trim Schedule)

When I say consistency, I'm focusing on doing certain work daily—and other work on a weekly basis. For example, I have designed my recording of podcasts, so I consistently record a podcast on a weekly basis.

How? I do the following:

- Record the podcast for 25 minutes. (I direct the material with myself and my co-host.)
- Have the audio editor cut the material down to 17 minutes.
- Listen to the first cut and direct the final edits so the material is 11 to 15 minutes in duration.

In this way, I ensure quality and still have a minimum of time invested.

Be sure to look at your weekly tasks from the perspective of *Design for Consistency.*

For example, you could choose to make your marketing phone calls on Tuesday. Every time Tuesday rolls around, you're prepared subconsciously to go directly to your desk and make the phone calls.

You could even use a slogan for the Tuesday phone calls. I've heard the phrase: 8 before 8 (that is, 8 phone calls before 8 AM) and 5 after 5 (5 phone calls after 5 PM).

A Big Advantage in Using a System

When you use a system, you change your experience of the world. You look upon yourself as more competent. You accomplish what I call *Behavior Change Through Incremental Evidence.* This process leads to a real improvement in personal confidence.

Trim Schedule

"You can help a thousand, but you can't carry three on your back." – Jim Rohn

With several clients, I use a process I call *A.C.T. Coaching.* Assess, Create, Trim. The Trim part is essential. We cannot simply add more to our schedule.

I emphasize "Discover the *best results your clients want."*

For your own schedule, ask yourself, "What are the best results I want?"

Use a System to Overcome Procrastination

In my workshops, I use the metaphor CPR (cardiopulmonary resuscitation) as I say, "We often need to use CPR in how we approach our time management."

In my system, the CPR stands for **Cue-->Preset Action -->Reward.**

If you want to accomplish more, think it through while the situation is cool, so you act automatically when the situation is hot.

For example, if you want to consistently do exercise in the morning, set out your running outfit on a chair next to your bed. Then, you automatically see the cue (running suit on chair) and go into action. Some people reward themselves with a morning cup of coffee—after exercising.

3. Say No with grace

One way to recover time is to free up your schedule. How can you do that? You learn to *say No with grace*.

We use the **3 G's of Saying No with Grace:**

3 G's
G – get away from the immediate "no"
G – go over your regret in your tone
G – give some "modest help"

Examples:
- G_1: "My schedule is rather full. I'll check. How about I get back to you at 4 pm on Thursday?"
- G_2: (express a big sigh) "I'm sad to say that my plate is full, and I can't be part of that—at this time."
- G_3: "How about we have a 10-minute phone call before your meeting? I could help you prepare. How does that sound?"

(As a side note: In Thailand, I replaced "say no with grace" with "set more leverage." Why? I was informed that the Thai culture encourages local people to avoid saying no.)

4. Energize Good, Excellent and Amazing

More than 20 years ago, I purchased a day planner. I found out that listing 20 tasks and carrying over 12 of them every day, turned the day planner into the binder of Guilt Lists.

Instead, we approach making a list with full empowerment. How?

We make 3 lists with the levels *Good, Excellent* and *Amazing*

- *Good* – these are the tasks that you're sure you can get done
- *Excellent* – these are tasks that require you to stretch a bit
- *Amazing* – these are the tasks that catapult you to a higher level (this level requires *Expanded Thinking*).

In Thailand, during my *Power Time Management* workshop, I demonstrated this process with three volunteers. I gave the first person 5 pencils and called this "Good"—to represent 5 phone calls (to place for marketing).

I gave the second person 10 pencils to represent the "Excellent" level.

I called for two more volunteers. I gave the third person the whole can of 40 pencils. I said, "This is Amazing! You're amazing."

The audience laughed at that one.

Then I took pencils out of the can and gave them to the two final volunteers.

I said, "This is called leverage. This is also called delegating."

Additional Insights about
Power Time Management

Personal Energy Paradox

One of my speeches is titled *Personal Energy Paradox: Your Path to Success—Better than Time Management*.

Here are some central elements of that speech:

I have observed that holding values like courage and compassion can give you "a star to steer by."

However, those values are high bars to live up to and

they can actually drain your personal energy. So, the Paradox is that having values that pull you forward like courage and compassion can also be the source of our beating ourselves up emotionally.

The solution to this is C&C—compassion and care. In particular, we're talking about self-compassion and self-care.

The important thing is to develop a buffer of extra energy. I call this your Personal Energy Buffer. You create such a buffer by scheduling breaks into your schedule.

My phrase is: *Take breaks or be broken.*

Using *Self-compassion*, you'll make sure to have a Personal Energy Buffer.

Self-compassion is a source of having extra energy. Compassion is defined as seeing suffering with the desire to relieve it. This is where self-care comes in. You do what's necessary to take care of yourself so that you're strong and you have more personal energy.

Final Bonus Material:

At my Facebook group known as "Leverage and Expand Your Success AND Happiness – with Tom Marcoux," I've written these #LeverageTips:

#LeverageTip: With a tough decision, look for "the sparkle" – the one element that "clicks" in your heart and points in the right direction.

#LeverageTip: I release fear. I'm growing & stretching. My True Self runs the show & fear is a quiet voice in the background.

#LeverageTip: When you face a point of "I don't know what to do next," know that you Are Growing and you're just about to Rise Up.

#LeverageTip: Take a Break to Be Brilliant. (Let your

creativity recharge.)

#LeverageTip: When someone says No, look for how your future has been Freed Up for a better experience.

#LeverageTip: Chip away every day.

- Friends: Many of us want to truly connect when we give a speech. A Facebook friend asked about closing a speech well. I replied: "I often give a 'final secret' wrapped in a brief story – with a phrase no more than six words long. *Story plus principle makes it memorable.*" Then I thought about how using humor warms up the audience – here are examples in my 2.3 min. video. .... many happy moments to you https://bit.ly/2EYEt6d

#LeverageTip: Remember "it's a show." (Your message must engage and entertain.)

I invite you to join my Facebook group "Leverage and Expand Your Success AND Happiness—with Tom Marcoux."

The best to you.

Reminder:
Get Access to Free Videos to Take Your Skills to a Higher Level
Go to GetTheBigYES.com/YourAdvantage

Succeed ™
Even If...

With Tom Marcoux
and Johanna E.

Episodes on YouTube
Podcast on iTunes

A Final Word and the Springboard

Congratulations on your efforts with this book.

Please consider continuing to work with me through my **executive coaching** (phone and in-person), workshops and keynote addresses. Visit my blogs:

PitchPowerFest.com

GetTheBigYES.com

YourBodySoulandProsperity.com

Enjoy my YouTube Channel *Success Even If* (podcast on iTunes).

Meanwhile, *to get even more value from this book,* take the plans and insights that you created and place them in some form in your calendar or day planner. *Plan and take action.* Return to these pages again and again to reconnect with the material and take your life to higher levels.

The best to you,

Tom

Tom Marcoux

Spoken Word Strategist

CEO, Executive Coach—Pitch Coach

Special Offer Just for Readers of this Book:

Contact Tom Marcoux at tomsupercoach@gmail.com for special discounts on coaching, books, workshops and presentations. Just mention your experience with this book.

Apply for a <u>FREE Breakthrough Strategy Session</u>—see the VIDEO at TomSuperCoach.com/breakthrough

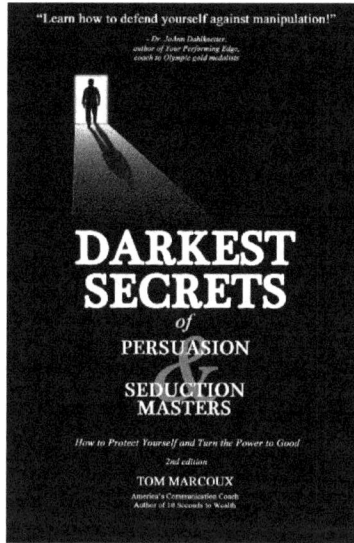

Excerpt from

Darkest Secrets of Persuasion and Seduction Masters: How to Protect Yourself and Turn the Power to Good

by Tom Marcoux, Spoken Word Strategist — Executive Coach
Copyright Tom Marcoux

. . . Now, I am in my 40's, with gray in my hair, and for 27 years I have been taking action to protect people.

And now is the time for me to protect you with the Countermeasures I reveal in this book.

Every human being needs to be able to break the trance that a Manipulator creates. You need to make good decisions, so you are safe, and you keep growing — and you are not cut down and crippled.

This Darkest Secrets material is so intense that I first released it only with the counterbalance of my most energizing and uplifting books, *Soar! Nothing Can Stop You This Year* and *Year of Awesome: How You Can Use 12 Success Principles including 10 Seconds to Wealth.*

An interviewer asked me: "Who can be the Manipulator?"

A co-worker, a boss, a salesperson, someone you're dating, and someone you think is a friend.

Now is the time—this very minute—for me to write this book to protect you.

I must speak the truth.

These Darkest Secrets of "persuasion masters" are …

Wait a minute! Let's say it plainly: These are the Darkest Secrets of masters of manipulation. Throughout this book, I will call these people what they are: Manipulators.

Dictionary.com defines "manipulate" as "To influence or manage shrewdly or deviously…. To tamper with or falsify for personal gain."

In this book, we will look on a manipulator as one who deviously influences someone with no concern about that person's well-being, and who causes harm to that person.

Here is the first Darkest Secret:

Darkest Secret #1:
Manipulators Make You Hurt
and Then Offer the Salve.

Manipulators would invite you to go out in the sun for hours and then sell you the salve to soothe your burns. The problem is that we don't notice that this is what they're doing.

For example, you're considering the purchase of a house. A Manipulator asks the question, "So, where would you put your TV?" This question is designed to put you into a trance.

Dictionary.com defines "trance" as "a half-conscious state, seemingly between sleeping and waking, in which ability to function voluntarily may be suspended." Let's condense this: In a trance, you may not be able to function freely.

Here is the second Secret:

Darkest Secret #2:

Manipulators Put You into a Trance.

To protect yourself, you must learn to use Countermeasures to Break the Trance.

All the Countermeasures (actions you can take to break the trance) in this book will make you stronger and more capable of protecting yourself.

Now, we'll view the third Secret:

Darkest Secret #3:

Manipulators Care Nothing for You and Human Decency: They'll lie, cheat, and do whatever they need to do so they win—but their charm masks all this.

Let's return to the example of a Manipulator selling you a house. A Manipulator does not pause for an instant to see if you can truly afford the new house. The Manipulator would neglect to mention that you will not only have your mortgage payment of $900. There will be additional costs: home repairs, property tax, water, electricity, homeowner's insurance, and more. The Manipulator only emphasizes what he or she knows you want to hear: "Look! $900 is better than the $1500 you're paying for rent, which is just going down the toilet. And the $900 is an investment."

Let's go back to **Darkest Secret #1:**

Manipulators make you hurt and then offer the salve.

The Manipulator has you feeling good about the solution (salve) and feeling bad about your current life situation.

How? A Manipulator will make you hurt through questions such as:

- What bothers you about paying $1500 a month for rent? (The Manipulator will use a derisive tone when he says the word *rent*.)
- What is *not* smart about paying rent on someone else's house instead of investing in your own

house?

- How do you feel about your children walking in the neighborhood where you live now?

Do you see how these questions are designed to make you hurt enough so that you'll buy?

An interviewer asked me, "Tom, aren't these good arguments for purchasing a house?"

"What we're looking at is the *intention* of the influencer," I replied. "Let's look at our definition of a manipulator as one who deviously influences someone with no concern about that person's well-being, and who causes harm to that person. If the person truly cannot afford the house, he or she will be harmed by buying it. If the manipulator conceals the truth, the manipulator is doing harm. That's the important difference."

Some friends of mine are ethical and helpful real estate agents who truthfully reveal the whole situation and help the purchaser achieve her own goals.

In this book, we are talking about another type of person; that is, unethical Manipulators.

* * *

In any given moment, we need to remember the tactics Manipulators use. We will focus on the word D.A.R.K. so you can remember details easily and protect yourself from Manipulators.

D — Dangle something for nothing

A — Alert to scarcity

R — Reveal the Desperate Hot Button

K — Keep on pushing buttons

1. Dangle Something for Nothing

What do conmen and conwomen do to seize your attention? They make you think you're getting a "steal."

I recently saw a documentary in which a conman on a street in England showed a toy that looked like it was dancing. This fake product was actually dancing because of a hidden, invisible thread. The conman was dangling something for nothing. The Entranced Buyer thought he was getting something worth $20 for only $5. That was the trick. The Entranced Buyer felt that he was getting $15 extra of value for his $5. What the Buyer really got was something worth nothing. Similarly, I know someone who purchased a copy of a Disney movie from a street vendor in San Francisco. She brought the copy home and it was unwatchable—and the street vendor was never seen again.

An old phrase goes, "A conman cannot con someone who is *not* looking for something for nothing."

How to Protect Yourself from "Dangle Something for Nothing"

Stop! Get on your cell phone and talk through the "deal" with someone you know who thinks clearly. Go home. Think about it. Do some research on the Internet. Listen to your gut feelings. If the salesman or conman is too insistent, get away from that Manipulator. Get quiet. Have a cup of water. Cool down. Break the Trance!

Break the Trance and Identify the Crucial Detail

Earlier, I mentioned that a Manipulator puts you into a trance. An added problem is that we put ourselves into a trance. For example, as you read this, are you thinking about your right toe? Most likely not (unless you stubbed your toe recently). The point is that we only focus on a tiny percentage of what is going on in our life.

Around fifteen years ago, I caused myself trouble because I put myself into a trance. I discovered that under certain conditions, friendship can make you nearly deaf. Here's how: I was producing a song for a motion picture. A good friend was singing backup in the chorus. Because of our friendship, I wanted him to sound great. I completely missed the Crucial Detail. In this kind of situation, the Crucial Detail is that what truly counts is how the lead singer sounds! I made a song that I could not release. What a waste of time and money! I had put myself into a trance.

In any situation in which the Manipulator is "dangling something for nothing," we often fall into a trance and miss the Crucial Detail. The most important detail is not that we're saving money if we order before midnight tonight. What counts is whether the product creates a lasting, crucial benefit in our lives. And is the benefit of the product worth the cost? Some people even program themselves to make mistakes by saying, "I can't pass up a bargain." The bargain is not the Crucial Detail.

Secrets to Break the Trance

This is the process of B.R.E.A.K.S. It will help you remember the proven methods to break a trance.

B — Breathe

R — Relax

E — Envision

A — Act on aromas

K — Keep moving

S — Smile

Secret #1: Breathe

Remember *Secret #1: Manipulators make you hurt and then offer the salve.* The Manipulator wants to put you into a state of being that fills you with a sense of urgency and anxiety. Oh, no! I'm going to miss the sale! Stop this highly vulnerable state. Take a deep breath.

End of Excerpt from *Darkest Secrets of Persuasion and Seduction Masters: How to Protect Yourself and Turn the Power to Good*
Purchase your copy of this book (paperback or eBook) at online retailers
See Free Chapters of Tom Marcoux's 47 books
at http://amzn.to/ZiCTRj

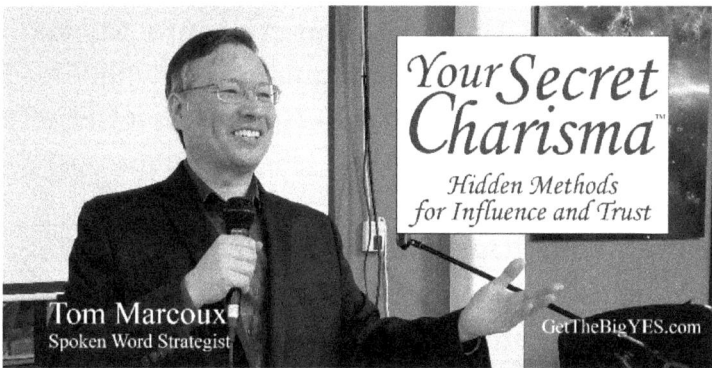

Better than About the Author
How Tom Marcoux Can Help You

When you want Real Confidence to Accelerate Your Success ... work with Tom Marcoux, the Spoken Word Strategist and Executive Coach. Need help to take the grand stage in the world?—with a pitch, new brand, a business, a TED Talk, speeches, video marketing, a book? Imagine your impact with all of these elements optimized for Your Leap Upwards to Success and Fulfillment. Tom Marcoux has built his expertise with his life journey. Tom won a special award at the EMMY AWARDS, and his feature film went to Cannes Film market. He taught MBA students at STANFORD UNIVERSITY. *The San Francisco Examiner* has designated

Tom Marcoux as "The Personal Branding Instructor." As a pro member of the National Speakers Association (over 19 years), He taught effective Pitch delivery to Stanford Entrepreneurs and Silicon Valley Entrepreneurs ... and more.

Methods You Can Trust

Tom Marcoux has coached thousands of CEOs, small business owners, startup founders, MBA students (Stanford University and other universities) and audiences. Author of over 50 books, Tom has two required textbooks for MBA students at Sofia University (on Authentic Marketing and Authentic Leadership Communication ... the leadership book is *Shape the Future, Lead Like a Pro*). As a CEO, Tom has led teams in the U.K., India and USA simultaneously.

Take the Grand Stage in the World

Tom helps with your Speech – Pitch – Video Marketing – Networking ... and rehearsing for your critical life-changing meeting. **Contact Tom at GetTheBigYES.com**

International Speaker Tom Marcoux has energized audiences from Silicon Valley, California to New York, Thailand, New Zealand and more.

Tom's Methods Empower Clients to Get Their Best Results

⇨ "I'm truly grateful to Tom Marcoux for essential tips that helped me win the Grand Prize of the Pitch Competition—the Igniter Summit in Bangkok, Thailand." – Neeraj Aggarwala, CEO/Founder of Sportido

⇨ "Tom Marcoux has coached me to make my speeches compelling and powerful. He's helping me prepare my TED Talk. Do your career a big favor and engage Tom Marcoux, the Spoken Word Strategist." – Dr. JoAnn Dahlkoetter, author of *Your Performing Edge* and

Coach to CEOs and Olympic Gold Medalists

⇨ "Tom Marcoux coached me to get more done in 10 days than other coaches in 2 years." – Brad Carlson, CEO of MindStrong, LLC

Your Next Steps

#1. See free Special Videos at GettheBigYES.com/nextstep

#2. Apply for a **Free Hidden Breakthrough Strategy Session** at GetTheBigYES.com/nextstep

#3. *Subscribe* to YouTube Channel *Succeed Even If* at https://bit.ly/2W9LaIf

#4. Hear Podcasts on iTunes *Succeed Even If* (over 50 podcast episodes on topics including enhance confidence, speak with no fear, and more)

#5 Look inside Tom's books at a major online retailer https://amzn.to/2Iq5WQl. Tom's books include
- *Soar with Confidence*
- *Darkest Secrets of Charisma*
- *Relax, You Don't Have to Sell: How You Can Make Sales Without Being Pushy*
- Over 47 more books

Even More *Best Results*

"Tom Marcoux coached me so well that when I faced a high-level prospective client, it was amazing. It was unbelievable how easy it felt to me. I wasn't nervous because Tom guided me through all the rehearsing. Tom emphasizes *'Words – Strategy – Rehearsal.'* I was more-than-ready because we had worked through all the possible scenarios. Tom also empowers me with his expertise with building a unique and compelling brand: logos, language, media releases, speech-writing, videos and more." – Tim Cox, the Business Systems Strategist

"Tom helped me unearth deeply emotional and humorous moments in my speech to move the hearts of the audience." – Krishna Noru

"Tom Marcoux has been an NAB Conference favorite [speaker] for six years. And he is very energetic." – John Marino, Vice President, National Association of Broadcasters, Washington, D.C.

One of Tom's books rose to #1 on Hot New Releases in Business Life (and in Business Communication)—at a major online retailer.

"Tom Marcoux helped me in ways no other coaches could. Anyone who has the opportunity to work with Tom is blessed for sure." – Junie Moon Schreiber

"Using just one of Tom Marcoux's methods, I got more done in 2 weeks than in 6 months." – Jaclyn Freitas, M.A.

Visit Tom at GetTheBigYES.com

www.ingramcontent.com/pod-product-compliance
Lightning Source LLC
Chambersburg PA
CBHW060534210326
41519CB00014B/3219